The Torch of Liberty

Also from Westphalia Press

westphaliapress.org

The Torch of Liberty

by Frederic Arnold Kummer

Illustrated by Kreigh Collins

WESTPHALIA PRESS

An imprint of Policy Studies Organization

Westphalia Press
An imprint of Policy Studies Organization
1527 New Hampshire Ave., NW
Washington, D.C. 20036
info@ipsonet.org

ISBN-13: 978-1-63391-062-1
ISBN-10: 1633910628

Cover design by Taillefer Long at Illuminated Stories:
www.illuminatedstories.com

Daniel Gutierrez-Sandoval, Executive Director
PSO and Westphalia Press

Rahima Schwenkbeck, Director of Media and Publications
PSO and Westphalia Press

Updated material and comments on this edition
can be found at the Westphalia Press website:
www.westphaliapress.org

THE TORCH OF LIBERTY

FREDERIC ARNOLD KUMMER

THE
TORCH
OF
LIBERTY

Illustrated by
Kreigh Collins

THE JOHN C. WINSTON COMPANY
Chicago   Philadelphia   Toronto

To

HELEN

with

LOVE AND GRATITUDE

for one who has never failed

CONTENTS

ILLUSTRATIONS

PROLOGUE

THE SPIRIT OF LIBERTY SPEAKS

I am the Spirit of Liberty. *By the light of my torch all who wander blindly in the shadows of fear and oppression can be set free.*

I hold aloft a beacon to guide men in the ways of reason and of justice, of honor and of truth—the ways of democracy, bringing peace and good will to earth.

Yet the road I point out is a perilous one, and upon its hard surface many millions have died.

Greed and cruelty and lust for dominion over other men lurk along its borders, hiding their faces behind lying masks, ever ready to strike the traveler down.

Century after century the struggle has gone on, but while at times the light of my torch has grown dim, no power of evil can extinguish its eternal flame.

Far back in the mists of the past a few wise men began to glimpse faintly my guiding light—seekers after truth who taught their followers that Kings and Emperors were but human beings like themselves, to be obeyed only so long as they used their powers justly.

But Kings and Emperors were strong, and the people weak,

so that none had the courage to oppose them. Not until the men of Hellas, of whom blind Homer sang, came down from their northern forests to build new homes in sunlit Greece did my torch begin to shine with brightest flame.

Here were a people free of soul who bowed their heads to none save leaders of their own choosing—men of a warrior race who were to write upon the pages of history a message of courage and truth and beauty so crystal clear that it has thrilled the heart of mankind for over two thousand years.

In the Greek city-states government by free peoples became a living and breathing thing, and democracy was born.

EAGLE'S FLIGHT

THE way through the mountain gorge seemed endless; even the younger men of the tribe shivered beneath the icy blasts.

In the northern forests from which they had come wood was always plentiful. Blazing fires on the hearths of their log houses kept everyone snug and warm during the long winter months. Here in these snow-covered passes, however, there were no trees fit for firewood, but only small, gnarled bushes, the limbs and twigs of which gave out a pale and cheerless flame.

For a week the tribe had struggled onward against the ice and snow that blocked their way, pushing the oxcarts through heavy drifts, camping around their small, makeshift fires, wondering when these hardships would be at an end.

3

In the high country north of the mountains they had come upon groups of shaggy herdsmen tending small flocks of goats. These natives, on being questioned in a strange tongue, shook their heads, waved the blond travelers southward as though to say that beyond the line of snow-capped peaks lay the fertile lands the wanderers sought. Now many among the tribesmen huddled in the shelter of their oxcarts began to think they had been purposely misled.

Snow fell that morning, and the sky was a dull slate gray, like the rocks. The shivering elders and the younger children, wrapped in their thick fur mantles, burrowed deep in the dry grass, the cattle fodder with which the oxcarts were filled.

About the campfires young women, strong and deep breasted, cooked bits of half-frozen meat over the pale flames, while men and youths fed the patient oxen or broke the ice on mountain pools with their axes to secure water for the camp.

All the folk of the tribe were tall and powerfully built, with clear blue eyes and long yellow hair the color of ripe corn. They wore stout sandals of oxhide laced with leather straps as far up as the knees. Their kirtles and tunics were made of heavy homespun cloth, fleece-lined and warm. Cloaks of bear- and wolfskin hung from their shoulders, held in place by bronze or silver clasps, and broad bands of the same metals around the arms of the fighting men served both as ornaments and as armor against an enemy's blows. Shields made of bull's hide, studded with bolts of iron or brass, were slung over their backs. Their leather helmets bore crests of oxhorns or the wings of eagles and other fierce birds of prey. Spears, swords, and heavy axes served them as weapons. To the small, dark goatherds of the hill country these mighty, fair-haired warriors had seemed like creatures of another world . . . giants, even gods.

This morning the tribe had halted to rest and take counsel since there seemed no way to go forward. The narrow, gloomy gorge they had been following for the past week was now blocked by a wall of rock and snow, with still more icy crags and peaks beyond. To add to their difficulties, Merax, headman of the tribe, lay ill in one of the oxcarts. A chill had come upon him during the night. He raved in strange madness, tearing at his breast, crying out that a fierce fire was consuming him in spite of the bitter cold.

Argos, son of Agamon, got up from the rock on which he had been sitting and shook the snow from his broad shoulders. He was called Argos because in the language of his tribe the word meant "swift." In all sports such as running, wrestling, climbing, as well as in the use of both spear and sword, he was quicker than any of the other young men.

Not far away Argos saw his father, one of the chief warriors and counselors of the tribe, talking with grim Urgo, mighty wielder of the ax, and Creon, the silver-tongued. They were standing beside the covered cart in which Merax lay, discussing his serious plight. From within the cart came the hoarse voice of their stricken leader shouting in his madness that the tribe should push on, that green fields and smiling valleys lay just ahead. By the gods of the forests, the streams, the mighty hills, he swore he would die rather than turn back from the way he had come.

Argos, listening, knew that food for both the folk and the cattle was almost gone. Their last spare ox had been killed and eaten. To slaughter more would mean they must abandon carts in which the children and the old people were being carried, along with the tribe's weapons and household gear. They were trapped in this narrow and dismal pass which, it now appeared, was not a pass at all, but a bitter, gloomy chasm with no out- let other than death.

But was this true? Argos, carrying his spear over one shoul- der, went to the far end of the defile. On either side towering walls of rock stretched upward, their icebound faces too steep to be climbed. Overhead a narrow slit of blue sky showed that the morning sun had pierced the snow clouds, but its rays did not find their way into the gorge.

Ahead lay only great masses of granite piled up as though by a giant's hand. Over this rocky wall Argos glimpsed more mountain peaks, white and glittering in the sun. But even if the stronger men of the tribe, the youths and warriors, could climb that icy barrier and escape from the gorge, no way was offered for the oxcarts with their burden of old people and children and the household goods that made up the wealth of the tribe. It seemed useless to attempt to go farther, yet Argos started to climb over the rocky wall.

Using his spear as a staff, he made his way slowly and care- fully up its jagged face. Many times higher than his head the barrier towered, but he kept on, cutting footholds in the hard-frozen snow with the blade of his spear, clinging to the slippery rocks, until at last he reached the crest of the wall and could see out over the valley beyond.

It was a harsh and frightening view, with snow and ice covering the steep slopes and ridges of rock like the backbones of huge skeletons stretching upward toward the farther peaks. If there were pleasant fields beyond those white-capped mountains, nothing was visible to indicate it from where Argos stood.

He rested for a time, breathing the keen, cold air. The climb over the rocks had set his young blood tingling. Although he still could not see the sun, the sky above him was clear, pale blue, the color of a robin's egg.

Suddenly he noticed a dark speck against the blue, moving high over the distant peaks, coming toward him. A bird . . . an eagle, he presently made out, flying back to some mountain nest with a young lamb in its talons.

At first this did not suggest anything to Argos' mind. It seemed natural enough for an eagle to carry off an ewe. Then another thought came to him. The great bird had flown from the south, and young lambs were not usually found amid the snow and ice of high mountains. Did this mean that somewhere beyond the shining peaks now facing him lay green fields with farms and sheepfolds and ewe lambs for eagles to steal? There was a deep gash in the line of the hills to the southward, but Argos could not see through it from where he stood. The granite shoulder of a pinnacle at his left cut off any forward view.

Inch by inch, foot by foot, he made his way over the ice-coated rocks, the treacherous crust of snow. In an hour he had covered a hundred yards, moving in a wide half-circle.

The struggle to keep his feet, to avoid a misstep which would plunge him into the valley below, tired even his lithe muscles. Had it not been for his spear, he could have made no progress at all. By forcing the blade of it into the hard-frozen snow he was able to swing from one perilous perch to another, and so at last reach the far side of the great granite shoulder.

There on a narrow, rocky ledge Argos paused, gave a shout of triumph. Far down the valley he could make out the opening in the line of distant hills—could glimpse through it broad verdant fields stretching away to the deep blue surface of the sea.

Here at last was the land of plenty his tribe had come so far to seek. A land, returning travelers had said, where the sun shone warm throughout all the year, where there was grass for the cattle, game for the huntsman, and golden fruits to be had for the picking. Beyond that narrow pass, which a thousand brave men might hold against an army, lay the country which was to be known as Greece.

Argos, thinking of his companions trapped in their icy, rock-walled gorge, was wondering how he might get them out. Not by the way he had come; only a few of the hardiest and strongest would be able to make that climb. He glanced down into the valley far below.

From the mouth of the pass a narrow winding road, little more than a goat track, led along the bottom of the valley, skirting the rocky bases of the hills. Upward it crawled, twisting and turning until it was lost in the peaks to the north.

This, Argos felt sure, was the way the tribe should have come. In some manner they had missed it, had wandered off to be trapped in that icy defile. If he could get down to the road below him, follow it back through the hills, he might be able to lead them to freedom.

From the narrow ledge on which he stood to the bottom of the valley stretched a slope strewn with rocks and so steep he wondered if he could ever descend it. Yet for a youth of cour' age there was but one course open: he must try. Setting the point of his spear in the snow, he swung off the narrow ledge.

The crusted snow beneath him was frozen too hard to give way under his weight although the blade of his spear easily pierced it. On that icy surface his feet flew out and he shot downward, clinging desperately to the weapon's stout ash haft.

For a moment the broad blade held, then it tore loose, but not until the speed of his fall had been somewhat checked. Using the spear as a rudder, Argos managed to guide himself toward one of the big gray boulders that projected above the sheet of frozen snow.

The shock, as he struck the boulder, nearly drove the breath from his body, but he was happily saved from death. He lay half stunned against the mass of rock, trying to regain his scat' tered senses.

Below, the glistening white surface of snow stretched fully a dozen spear'lengths to the next outcropping boulder. Instead of attempting to slide, Argos descended it methodically, cutting footholds with the blade of his spear. So from rock to rock he made his way toward the foot of the slope.

Now he was almost to the road. But from here on his path led straight downward, a vertical wall of rock as high as six men stretched between him and the valley below. He took off his wolfskin coat and with a hunting knife cut the leather into narrow strips. These he knotted together to form a rope. One end he made fast to a rock. When he tossed the other from the edge of the cliff, it reached little more than halfway to the bottom.

Hurling his spear ahead of him, Argos swung over the side of the cliff, checking his downward progress by the knots in the rope. At last he let go and crashed heavily into a clump of pine bushes at the base of the rock. Bruised and shaken, but not seriously hurt, he staggered to his feet, and having recov' ered his spear, started up the winding road.

Higher and higher it rose, twisting snakelike through the hills. As he rounded one of its many turns, he came face to face with three of the small, shaggy men he had seen in the upland country tending their herds of goats. They were armed with short swords and javelins and carried round brazen shields upon their backs. Except for the small hunting knife, Argos' only weapon was his spear.

He stood in the middle of the roadway gripping it, waiting for the three to attack. They cried out sharply in words he did not understand. They seemed astonished by Argos' great

Frightened by the yellow-haired giant's courage, he turned and
fled like a scared rabbit.

height, his wide, powerful shoulders, the long, yellow hair that shone like a golden mane in the sun. Then, recovering from their first surprise, they swung shields about and came on in a rush, their javelins raised.

Argos carried no shield, having left it behind for easier climbing over the rocks. One of the three men, braver than his fellows, led the charge several feet in advance. With a cry he hurled his javelin, sent it spinning like a shaft of light at Argos' breast.

Well had Argos been named "swift." In that perilous moment he sprang to one side and the deadly dart flashed harmlessly past his shoulder. The man who had flung it came on, drawing his sword. Argos thrust the point of his spear downward. The charging man tripped over it and sprawled headlong in the road.

Instantly Argos bent down, tore the shield from the fallen man's arm. The small, round target gave him a means of defense. As his two remaining opponents hurled their javelins, he caught the light darts upon it then leaped forward to attack. The first man he felled to the ground with a mighty sweep of his shield. The second, frightened by this yellow-haired giant's fierce courage and speed, took to his heels, running like a scared rabbit in the direction of the pass.

The warrior who had tripped and fallen was on his feet again. Turning, Argos charged him, spear raised. After one look at its broad, shining blade, the fellow took after his companion. For a space Argos pursued him, then remembered the man in his rear, the one he had dashed to the ground with a blow of his shield. The fallen man, crawling forward, had recovered his javelin from the edge of the road. As Argos wheeled to face him, he flung it. The slender dart sang swiftly through the air.

Before Argos had time to protect himself, its bright point struck. He felt a sudden pain in his side. The javelin had pierced him through and through. Its red point showed a palm's breadth beyond his back. He staggered to the rocky wall that bordered the road and leaned against it, supporting himself with his spear. The small, shaggy warrior, seeing that his opponent was wounded, cried out in triumph but dared not come closer for fear of that spear's broad blade. Instead he contented himself with hurling a second javelin, recovered from the snow. This Argos turned aside with a twist of his shield. He was dizzy from pain, but unless he fell, the dark-haired warrior would not dare to come closer.

Argos glanced downward. At his feet lay the javelin that had just been turned back by his shield. Gritting his teeth, he stepped forward, snatched it up, and before the man facing him realized it had flung the dart swift and true.

It pierced the dark-haired warrior's shoulder, above the brazen rim of his shield. With a howl of pain the fellow ran off after his comrades down the road.

For many minutes Argos waited, fearing they might come back. His eyes followed the narrow, rocky trail as it wound up through the hills toward the higher ground above. These dark-haired men dwelt beyond the mountains, on stony slopes to the north. This steep winding road must lead there since down it they had come. Argos hoped that if he could make his way back along the trail, he might again rejoin his people and free them from their high, rocky trap.

He stepped into the road and found at once that he could not move without dreadful pain so long as the dart remained in his side. Bracing himself against the rocks, he tore it free. A stream of blood stained the snow at his feet. At every move-ment fresh bleeding occurred. He loosened the broad leather belt around his waist and raised it higher, drawing it tight over the wound. He hoped this pressure against his fleece-lined tunic might check the flow of blood. Then, swallowing a handful of snow, he set out up the long winding road.

In the narrow defile where the tribe had camped, all was sadness and gloom. Merax, their chieftain, lay dying.

The fever that struck him during the night had grown worse. By the time the noon sun brought a few cheering rays into the gorge he had closed his eyes forever, with a sigh of joy, thinking from the sunlight that he had brought his people to the golden land they sought.

The women and the children sat huddled drearily about their campfires while the warriors and elders met to decide who should lead them now that Merax was dead.

His body lay in the first of the long line of oxcarts and around it, in a cleared space, the fighting men stood, muttering among themselves that the fates were against them since their leader had been stricken down in their hour of need.

One of the elders, a fragile graybeard, spoke to the people.

"Men of Hellas," he said in a quavering voice, "by the will of the gods our chieftain, mighty Merax, has been taken from us to dwell forever with the shades' of his fathers in the Isles of the Blest. Now, as is the right and duty of free men, we meet to choose a new leader, bearing in mind that grave dangers are to be faced. The fates have frowned upon us in our journey, have led us to this evil place. Only a chieftain who is both stout of heart and wise in deed can save us from destruction. Let us therefore take counsel together, invoking the favor of the gods that we may choose aright!" The old man raised his eyes toward the heavens. "Now may great Zeus, the Father, and all the lesser gods of Earth and Sky and Wind and Sea grant us their blessing in this hour!"

The warriors about him clashed swords on shields, lifting their weapons high.

"Great Zeus, favor us!" they chanted.

Another of the elders addressed the gathering—a small, bent man leaning on an ashen staff.

"I speak for Creon, the Silver-Tongued," he said. "What braver or wiser chieftain can we find to lead us?"

"Creon! Creon!" some of the people cried.

A grim-eyed warrior faced the circle of fighting men.

"We are caught in a trap," he muttered. "One would need the wings of an eagle to escape from it! Our stomachs are empty! Our women, our children, our cattle cry out to be fed! Before we choose Creon as our leader, let him tell us what he will do to save the people from death!"

Now Creon, stepping quickly forward, spoke.

"You ask me, Zetes, what I would do to save the people from death? Thus do I answer you. I would turn the oxcarts around and start toward the north whence we came, taking food from the hill tribes and others along the way. So we shall once more win back to our forest homes. To stay here is to die. What say you, men of Hellas? Shall a wise man break his head against a stone?"

The rattle of swords upon shields became louder and many found the words of Creon good. But one of the younger warriors, stepping forward, spoke scornfully.

"Have we come these many leagues, O Hellenes, to turn aside like beaten dogs because we lack food to eat? What shall our wanderings profit us if now we creep back empty-handed to our homes? Let Urgo the Strong lead us! He is one to show the way!"

At this challenge many of the younger warriors cried out their approval, shouting Urgo's name.

He stood forth, the mightiest axman in the tribe. Wielding that huge weapon he was the equal of three ordinary fighting men.

"I hold with Creon," he cried in a deep voice. "We should turn the oxcarts around since in this place none may live. But I like not his plan to go back to our forests. Let us instead fall with ax and sword upon these dark people of the hills, taking from them their goats, their lands, their houses. Though the country in which they dwell be poor, we shall yet have food for our bellies, wood for our fires, fields in which our cattle may graze. Our people have grown weary of wandering. Why not settle down in these nearby hills, slaying any who would oppose us? So I would do, men of Hellas."

The younger warriors, eager for battle, clashed their weapons, making a loud clamor.

"Urgo! Let Urgo lead us!" they cried.

Now another of the elders stepped forward. His voice was as thin and sharp as the blade of a hunting knife. His eyes were as blue as ice.

"Creon hath wisdom," he said, "but is lacking in courage since he counsels naught save retreat! Urgo, while stout of heart, offers only battle with unknown tribes in which we may all be slain. In this hour of danger we should choose a leader who is both wise and brave. I name Agamon. Let him stand forth and speak!"

Now Argos' father, Agamon, addressed the people. As tall as Urgo, but less powerfully built, he faced the circle of warriors confidently. His eyes were clear and untroubled. His forehead, beneath thick red-brown hair, was calm and serene.

"Men of Hellas," he began, "as Creon hath said, we are in grave danger here in this narrow snowbound gorge. We cannot go forward because of the wall of rock. But does that mean we must needs turn back? Are there not other ways to right and left? Those wanderers who returned to our forest homes told of rich, golden lands beyond those icy peaks. Are we then ready to say there is no road to such lands because we have failed to find one? Having come thus far, shall we in despair give up our quest? Is that the way of brave men?"

"No! No!" came in a roar from the crowd.

"First," Agamon went on, "let us send out to either side those amongst us who still have strength to brave ice and snow and perilous rocks to seek the road we have missed. A score of our stoutest young men who do not fear suffering or death! Such a road there must be, else travelers could not have reached these golden lands nor come back to tell us their tale."

The circle of warriors nodded, finding logic in what Agamon had said. But their stomachs were empty, their bodies chilled by cold.

"Even brave men must eat," one grumbled.

Agamon turned on him, smiling.

"Tonight the oxen of Merax' cart shall be slaughtered," he said, "that all may have their fill. The wood of his wagon we will burn for our fires, that all may keep warm. If, tomorrow, a way be not found, more cattle must be slain."

"Without oxen," a grizzled warrior objected, "how shall the carts for the elders and the children be drawn?"

"If oxen be lacking," Agamon replied angrily, "let us draw them ourselves! And if the way prove too steep for carts to travel, then we will carry those who lack strength to walk. If we must perish, let it be not as cowards, but as brave men!"

Many in the circle of warriors cried out in agreement, but others shook their heads, eyeing fearfully the tall cliffs and the snow-clad mountains that hemmed them in. Then Creon spoke winged words.

"Now is the season in our homeland," he said, "when the ice will be gone from the rivers and the lakes. The trees in the forests will be clothed in young green, and all the fields will smile in the sun. The women will be singing over their looms; the young maidens will deck their hair with flowers. There will be fat kine in the meadows and fat geese in the pens. Let us go back to our people, for only thus can our strength be restored. Then—on another day, another year—we may again set forth. It is no sign of courage to belittle dangers we may not overcome, nor of a coward, to turn from them when the gods have denied us their favor. Look!" Creon pointed to the sky. A flock of gray geese was winging northward. "An omen, showing us the way we should go! Let us, too, fly from these bitter mountains back to our homeland. Here we shall find naught but death!"

A great cheering came from the cold and hungry tribe. In every heart Creon had set a picture of their far-off homes that warmed them. The brave words of Agamon were for the moment forgotten as they gazed about the cheerless, rocky gorge. Then Agamon spoke again.

"It may be that Creon has not read the omen aright," he said. "Geese flying northward in the spring must needs come from sunnier, warmer lands. Mayhap the gods seek to tell us that beyond these icy peaks lie the pleasant fields and streams these swift, gray birds have left. This may be an omen to urge us on. . . ."

Now clamor broke out among the tribesmen, some saying one thing, some another. Some ranged themselves at Creon's side, urging that he be made chief. Others, fewer in number, gathered about Agamon. A third and still smaller group upheld Urgo, these being the fiercest of the warriors, who wished neither to return to their homes nor to stay where they were. But many wavered, and as the cold blasts of evening swept through the gorge they began by twos and threes to leave Urgo's banner, some joining those about Creon, others ranging themselves at Agamon's side. Each moment the number of Creon's followers increased. A few more and the choice would be made.

Suddenly, from the campfires farther along the gorge, came the sound of women's voices raised in shrill excitement. Thinking the camp had been attacked, the warriors sprang forward, waving their axes and swords.

For what seemed to Argos unending hours he toiled in agony up the winding trail. At times the pain from his wound was so great that he felt unable to take another step, but the fear that if he should die there the tribe might not be saved drove him on.

Over and over the tightly bound belt about his loins slipped down and blood oozed afresh from his wound. Gritting his teeth he set it in place again, binding the broad leather girdle against his fleece-lined tunic until he could scarcely breathe.

Once, losing consciousness, he fell by the roadside and in his weakness slept until still sharper pain from the wound roused him. Moistening his lips with a handful of snow, he dragged himself up the last steep rise on hands and knees.

Here the narrow trail he had been following joined a somewhat more level road. At the side of it Argos saw the bones of slaughtered animals, the deep ruts made by the wheels of wagons, the hoof marks of oxen in the snow. They pointed in one direction only—toward the south. A wave of triumph swept over him. He shouted for joy.

This was the road by which the tribe had traveled on its way into the gloomy gorge beyond, and, in so doing, had missed the half-hidden trail that led down to the pass. He must reach his comrades before they perished of hunger in their icy trap.

Filled with this thought, Argos drove himself on. How far it was to the camp he did not know, but the distance could not be great. Already steep rocks, rising on either side of him, marked the beginning of the gorge. He remembered having passed them during the late hours of the afternoon before. In the dying light of day, none of the tribe had seen, much less thought to explore, the winding trail up which he had just come.

Weak and dazed, he struggled forward, every step bringing with it a stab of pain. At last he reached the line of oxcarts, staggered past them, supporting himself upon his spear.

Some of the women, huddled about their brush fires, cried out in alarm as Argos appeared. Pale and bloodstained, his fair hair matted with sweat and dirt, his eyes staring, he suggested a ghostly figure from the nether world.

Unmindful of the women's cries, Argos stumbled toward the group of elders and fighting men now hurrying from their deliberations to discover the cause of the alarm. He saw his father and went to him, swaying from weakness.

"I've found the way out . . . the way to the golden lands!" he cried proudly and fell to his knees in the snow.

Agamon raised the youth in his arms and carried him to one of the wagons. The sharp-voiced elder who had first proposed Agamon's name hobbled forward, waving his staff.

"If indeed the road has been found," he shouted, "what chieftain shall lead us? Creon, who would have turned back? Urgo, whose hope lay in robbing and slaying the dark people of the hills? Or Agamon, whose counsels have now been shown true by his brave son? Choose, men of Hellas! The gods have spoken!"

"Agamon!" the warriors, the people roared. The clamor was so great that Argos, hearing it, raised his head.

"Hail, Chieftain!" he murmured to his father, then sank back, smiling, upon his bed of furs.

That night great fires blazed in the gorge as the massive timbers of Merax' cart were burned. His slaughtered oxen provided a feast for the tribe that sent them to rest with new warmth in their bodies and new hope in their hearts. Argos, his wound bound up, his strength refreshed by cups of hot juices from the roasting meat, slept soundly in spite of the pain in his side. He was too worn out to feel it.

In the morning, after Merax had been laid with his weapons in a rock-piled tomb, all the carts were turned around and started down the winding trail toward the pass. Argos, propped in the front of his father's wagon, pointed out the way. Where it proved unduly steep, warriors held back the huge, solid wheels of the carts so that the stumbling oxen might not be overrun. By midafternoon they reached the narrow gap in the hills. Here, beyond a gray crag at the edge of a tumbling stream, they stood in silence for a long moment, then broke into triumphant cheers.

Before them lay a wide, green country, rolling in gentle slopes down to the sea. Fields of rich emerald, drenched by the sun; tall oaks and slender cypress trees; clumps of wild olives and dark pines. Blue water beyond, streaked with turquoise and amethyst, flecked with white foam.

Argos, gazing at the scene from his bed in the cart, lay silent, too full of emotion to speak. His father smiled at him, then turned to the excited people.

"We are given, O men of Hellas, a fair, new land in which to build our homes! Let us make it a land of brave, free men where none shall kneel in homage save to the immortal gods!"

For a thousand years I held my torch high over the land of the Hellenes, the land of the Greeks.

I saw these blue-eyed warriors sweep aside the small, dark men of the Mediterranean Sea, taking their cities, their culture, building anew. I watched Troy fall, saw Leonidas and his gallant Spartans hold at bay the hordes of Persian Xerxes until a traitor crept through the mountain passes to stab Greek heroes in the back. I looked on, weeping, as fair Athens fell before the Asian's might but dried my tears when Persian power was broken by sea at Salamis, and the cause of democracy triumphed over a Conqueror's sword.

Happily I saw burnt Athens rise again, statelier, more beautiful than before. Under the benign influence of a government in which every free man possessed a vote, I saw great minds flourish and genius come to its fullest and finest flower. Philosophers, poets and playwrights gave their sublime thoughts to the world; men of science delved deep into nature's laws, while architects and sculptors wrought new beauty in marble and bronze. Plato, Phidias and Praxiteles, Socrates, Pythagoras and Aristophanes—not all the Kings and Emperors of the past, ruling men by force, had created a thousandth part of what Greece in the days of her glory gave to mankind. To show for their efforts, the Conquerors had only ruined cities, starving peoples, mounds of empty skulls. Here at Athens, during the Golden Age of Pericles, I saw men, freed from ancient fears and cruel tyrannies, rise to heights of mind and body unknown to the world before. Here was liberty. Here was democracy, brave and triumphant.

DEMOCRACY TRIUMPHANT

THE groves of cypress and laurel trees looked cool and inviting, and Alcamenes stepped from the dusty road to seek refuge for a while in its shade.

Within the ring of trees he found a small, clear pool. Putting aside his heavy pack he knelt down and drank thirstily of the fresh, sparkling water.

There were bread and meat in the pack, and Alcamenes proceeded to eat his midday meal. Afterward, he stretched out on the mossy bank to rest. He had walked steadily since daybreak, and he was tired.

A frog, perched on a rock at the far side of the pool, caught his eye. The creature's fat body and solemn, dignified stare made him think of a dull and portly politician.

Smiling, he drew a lump of moist clay from his pack and begin to model an image of the frog. He worked quickly, deftly, using a small tool made of polished olivewood to shape the finer details of the figure. Except for his swiftly flying fingers he kept very still, lest some sudden movement on his part might alarm the creature and send it plunging into the water.

The road and the fields beyond it lay hot in the noonday, sun, but within the little grove only occasional rays came through the over-arching canopy of leaves to fleck the surface of the pool with a pattern of gold. Alcamenes had just begun work on the frog's webbed feet when loud voices from the road drove his model headlong from its perch. He glanced through the tangle of laurel branches and saw a man running toward the grove, followed by two others, armed with clubs.

The first man, brown-bearded and middle-aged, set his back against one of the trees along the roadside and drawing a short, brass-hilted sword prepared rather clumsily to defend himself. His assailants, a pair of unkempt, scowling ruffians, ran toward him, loudly demanding that he surrender his pack. Bandits from the hills, Alcamenes decided, and leaped swiftly into the road.

He was tall for his age, and well built, The muscles of his sunburned body rippled smoothly beneath his sleeveless woolen tunic. Surprised by his sudden appearance, the two ruffians hesitated for a moment then turned on him with uplifted clubs.

Alcamenes, well skilled in Olympic games and sports, charged the first of the two bandits impetuously. Bending low to avoid a blow from the man's club, he seized him about the waist in a wrestler's hold and with a dexterous twist of the knee sent the fellow sprawling.

Meanwhile, the traveler at the tree sprang forward, brandishing his sword, whereupon the second of the two ruffians, finding himself assailed from behind, turned and fled down the road. His defeated companion, staggering to his feet, promptly followed him. Alcamenes glanced after them, grinning.

"I seem to have arrived at a fortunate moment," he said.

"Yes." The brown-bearded traveler sheathed his sword. "I fear I am no warrior, and these rascals would easily have taken my pack—and no doubt cracked my pate in the bargain." He glanced toward the leather pouch that hung from his shoulders. "However," he went on, smiling, "they would have been disappointed in their booty, since I carry naught worth stealing."

Alcamenes pointed to the circle of trees behind him.

"Come into the grove and refresh yourself with a draught of cool water."

The traveler followed him to the edge of the pool. As he bent down to drink he caught sight of the small clay frog. For a long moment he examined it.

"How did this come here?" he asked.

"I modeled it," Alcamenes said. "To amuse myself, while resting after my midday meal. You think it good?"

"Very good. Excellent. You are, I see, a sculptor."

"At least," Alcamenes admitted diffidently, "I hope to become one. There are friends at home who think I have talent."

The second ruffian, finding himself attacked from the rear, turned and fled.

"You live nearby?" the brown-bearded man went on, forgetting in his interest the drink of water he had knelt to take.

"No. I come from the island of Lemnos, in the Aegean Sea."

"A long journey."

"Yes. I worked my passage by trading ship to the Locrian coast and am now on the way to Athens."

"And what seek you in Athens?"

"Work, that I may live. And a chance to learn something more of the sculptor's art. In that great city there are many, I am told, who would teach me."

The bearded stranger smiled, his blue eyes twinkling.

"The figure you have made of the frog," he said, "shows much skill. With a few broad strokes you have caught the small creature's soul. At Athens you will find not only masters to teach you, but beauty to inspire you. In deciding to go there I think you have made a wise choice."

"It was not an easy one," Alcamenes muttered, frowning. "My father, who is a man of importance on our Isle of Lemnos, opposed my design. He fought against the Persians at Marathon and wished me to become a soldier like himself."

"I see." The stranger picked up the bit of olivewood that Alcamenes had dropped beside the figure of his frog. "With such a small weapon as this," he went on, smiling, "a man may conquer more worlds than have ever been won by the sword. What victory did great Xerxes gain to set beside the Winged Victory of Paeonius?"

"Such has been my thought," Alcamenes agreed eagerly.

"Those who bring war create nothing; their only mission is to destroy."

"As the Persians destroyed Athens, leaving free men to re-build it more beautiful than before. Only in peace can great works of art be produced. All the conquerors of the world could not give us so much as a single line of poetry, a worth-while statue, a clever play. They leave behind them only ruins and dead men's bones. In Athens men live free, under the leadership of wise Pericles."

"Even in far-off Lemnos," Alcamenes said, "I have heard of the glory he has brought the Athenian State and its people."

"He is a true friend of all who labor, whether it be with hand or with brain. Yet for all his greatness, one of the kindest and simplest of men."

"You know him then?"

"Very well. We are indeed close friends. I am myself a citi-zen of Athens."

Alcamenes stared doubtfully at the stranger's worn and travel-stained clothing, his dusty shoulder pack. This wanderer of the roads a friend of Pericles, head of the great Athenian city-state? It seemed incredible.

"What brings you here, to Phocis?" he questioned. "So far from home?"

"Not so far, as the crow flies." The stranger chuckled, twist-ing his crisp brown beard. "Only a three days' journey—four at the most. I have been on a visit to Delphi and am now returning. . . ."

"Delphi? You mean the place where the Oracle speaks? Fore-telling the future? Is it nearby?"

"Yes." The bearded traveler pointed between the laurel branches. "Those high, shining hills you see to the east are the peaks of Parnassus. Delphi lies at their feet. A road called the Sacred Way leads up to the shrine of the Sibyl, where many fine temples and statues are to be seen. Some of the statues are my work," the stranger added, smiling. "I, too, am a sculp-tor."

"You?" Alcamenes was suddenly embarrassed. "Then I hold it a strange bit of chance, that we should meet. What is your name?"

"Phidias," the bearded man said. "And yours?"

Alcamenes flushed bright red to his ears; he could with diffi-culty mumble a coherent reply. Phidias! Even in Lemnos that name was known. The greatest sculptor in Greece!

"Phidias? Tramping the roads!" he muttered.

"Why not?" The sculptor laughed. "I am a plain man. All artists are, or should be. I walk because it pleases me to see the country—and the exercise aids digestion. Do you think, because I am Phidias, that I should travel like some Persian satrap, riding on an elephant?"

Alcamenes, still scarlet, picked up his clay frog and tossed it into the pool.

"My name is Alcamenes," he said, "and I have chattered to such as you about my foolish dreams."

Phidias laid his hand gently on the young man's arm.

"You have also saved me from a cracked pate at the hands of two thieving ruffians. In return for that, I shall help make your dreams come true. Work I can promise you, along with my other pupils. There are many stones yet to be shaped for the Parthenon. Beyond that your own talents must carry you, as with every man. The future lies in your hands." Phidias, sweeping aside Alcamenes' attempts to thank him, rose. "Let us go forward now toward our journey's end. There are still many leagues ahead of us. Come." He led the way to the road.

Alcamenes, shouldering his pack, followed, and the two travelers turned southward in the direction of Thebes and of Athens. A pleasant breeze from the Gulf of Corinth tempered the heat of the afternoon. Overcome by the fame of his companion, Alcamenes said little, but as they went along, Phidias spoke enthusiastically of the glory Pericles had brought to the Athenian State.

"Now at last," he said, "we have a leader who understands the true purpose and meaning of democracy. In the past, too great power has been given to those in high places, while the needs and wishes of the people have been ignored. Pericles looks on the State as a public enterprise, in which everyone should take part. He holds that since it is supported by the efforts and the taxes of all the people, all should share in its rewards. Thus, there are many in Athens who cannot afford to attend our splendid performances of music and the drama. For these, Pericles has set aside a special fund upon which poorer citizens may draw for that purpose, so all may share equally in the cultural life of the community. Again, consider the matter of public officials. For the first time, judges, magis-trates, even those who are called for jury duty, receive pay for their services. The same is true of the army and the navy; for Pericles holds that while our citizen-soldiers, being free and self-disciplined, display greater valor than the fighting men of despots, yet they too are public servants and should be paid like any others. Instead of surrounding himself with the rich and powerful, who would seek their own interests, Pericles chooses as his counselors and advisors such men as Sophocles, the poet, Herodotus, the historian, and Ictinus, the architect who has designed so many of the splendid buildings which crown the Acropolis. Even I," Phidias went on modestly, "have been given a part in the great work of beautifying the city. I am honored that Pericles calls me friend."

"Such a man," Alcamenes murmured, "should enjoy the friendship of all."

"He should, yes." Phidias made a swift gesture. "But as you grow older, my friend, you will learn that no man may achieve greatness without creating enemies who, through envy and jealousy, will seek to strike him down. There are such, even in Athens. A few selfish and unscrupulous politicians who resent the favor Pericles has gained with the people. Unable to attack him directly, they have struck at his friends. Thus An-axagoras, the great astronomer and mathematician, has been accused of atheism because he teaches that the sun is a flaming globe around which our earth revolves. So too has the incomparable Aspasia been attacked, because she is Pericles' friend. Only last year base rumors were started, claiming that the spending of money to beautify the Acropolis was a misuse of public funds. I myself heard the reply Pericles made to that charge. 'If the people of Athens wish my name, instead of theirs,' he said, 'to be graven upon these temples, I will myself defray the builders' cost!' But these attacks are only the stings of wasps and scorpions. Never has Athens been so happy, so contented, so strong. Rightly do men say that Pericles has brought the city a golden age."

Alcamenes, enthralled, listened to what the famous sculptor told him. He could scarcely wait to have his first view of Athens. Yet when, toward the evening of the fourth day, he stood on a broad, level plain gazing up at the heights of the Acropolis, the beauty and grandeur of the scene left him breathless.

Far above the city itself rose the great rock. Its graceful shrines and majestic temples, gleaming in white and gold and multicolored splendor, made him think of a jeweled crown.

A superb flight of marble steps led up to the heights, guarded at its top by a bronze figure of Athene as tall as six men. From all over the countryside and far out at sea the great figure of the goddess was visible, keeping watch over the city, her helm and spear and buckler shining in the sun like bright gold. But of all the sights upon that terraced hilltop, Alcamenes was most deeply stirred by the matchless beauty of the temple of Athene Parthenos—the Parthenon.

"The architect Ictinus," he heard Phidias saying at his elbow, "designed the building. To me has been entrusted its decora- tion, as well as the carving of the statue of Athene which it enshrines. As you see, the sculptures for the pediment, the great frieze which runs about all four sides of the building above the columns, are still incomplete. On those, assisted by my pupils, I am now at work. You will meet some of them at my house. Come, or we shall be late for the evening meal."

Alcamenes, humble at the thought that he too might have some share in that wonderful task, followed Phidias along the Street of the Tombs to the tall Double Gate at the city walls. By narrow, winding ways they came at length to a large market square, lined by many handsome buildings. This, Phidias told him, was the Agora, where, from a marble rostrum, Athenian leaders addressed the people when questions of public policy arose, allowing all, even the humblest citizen, to take part in the discussions.

In a narrow street not far from the Agora Phidias stopped before a painted doorway set in a low, windowless wall.

"Here is my home," he said, opening the door.

Beyond the door a stone-paved hallway led to the atrium, a pleasant place open to the sky with a fountain at the center. Passing through this, Phidias conducted Alcamenes into a grassy yard, about which lay many blocks of stone. From a long, low shed at the farther side of the yard came the sound of laughter, the ring of hammers, the voice of someone singing a gay, light song.

"My workshop," Phidias said, waving toward the shed. "Most of my pupils live here; I shall be glad to number you among them. Agoracritis!" he called.

A slender young man with curling dark hair came running from the shop, followed by half a dozen others.

"Welcome home, Master!" he shouted joyfully. His companions joined in the greeting.

"I bring a new pupil," Phidias said. "By name, Alcamenes. He hails from Lemnos, and will assist us in our work. Take him therefore among you, as a brother in the search for beauty and truth."

The youth named Agoracritis nodded. He had, Alcamenes thought, a very winning and humorous smile.

"Come along into the shop," he said, as Phidias turned back to the atrium. "We were just getting ready to eat our evening meal."

Alcamenes followed him. About the shed stood several large slabs of marble, upon which figures in relief were in process of being carved. Panels for the frieze, Alcamenes decided, noticing the small clay models beside each stone. The floor of the room was covered with chips and marble dust. There were large openings in the roof to admit light, but now, with the approach of evening, the place was growing dim.

Some of the students lit oil lamps. Others brought wooden trays and platters, containing cheese, barley cakes, dried figs, olives, jars of thin, red wine, placing them on a long, bare table. Pulling up their wooden stools, the group sat down to eat. All were curious to learn how Phidias, whom they called "The Master," had come to meet Alcamenes, and listened eagerly to his account of the ruffians' attack and the fight in the road.

"We all tell him," Agoracritis said, "that this habit of wan- dering about the country alone is a dangerous one, but he won't stop it. He claims that carrying nothing of value he has nothing to fear. But suppose thieves don't discover his pack is empty until they've knocked out his brains? What then?"

The young men laughed a great deal over their simple meal and Alcamenes felt curiously at home. It was a feeling that never left him during his long stay beneath the great sculptor's roof.

The sun was hot upon the heights of the Acropolis, and Alcamenes, who had been watching a group of workmen set one of the panels of the frieze in place, stepped into the shade of the long row of columns.

This frieze depicted a processional in honor of Athene, and since it extended around the great temple for a distance of over five hundred feet, the carving of its many panels was a tre- mendous task.

Seeing that the work of raising the stone was well in hand, Alcamenes went around to the front of the building and stepped into its dim, cool interior.

Facing him, at the great temple's rear, was the shrine, guarded by two rows of Doric columns, in which stood the statue of Athene. All the flesh parts of the figure were made

of polished ivory; the robes of pure gold. In her right hand the
Goddess held a winged Victory; her left, clasping the shaft of
a spear, rested lightly upon the rim of a huge circular shield.
Alcamenes had seen the great statue many times before during
the three years that had passed since his coming to Athens, but
he never tired of looking at it. Not only did the beauty of the
figure always thrill him, but he took an added pride in the fact
that it was the work of his beloved Master. During those years,
a deep affection had sprung up between Phidias and his new
and brilliant pupil. Except for Agoracritis, Alcamenes was the
only one to whom the Master would entrust the execution in
marble of his finest designs; would even permit, now and then,
to model figures, panels of his own.

As Alcamenes stood drinking in the beauty of the statue he
heard the sound of footsteps behind him and saw two men
approaching the shrine. They moved stealthily, not seeing the
young sculptor standing among the shadows. For a moment
they stared at the towering figure of the Goddess, then fixed
their gaze upon her great shield. On it was depicted a battle
between Greeks and Amazons.

One of the men pointed an accusing finger.

"His own portrait!" he muttered, indicating the sculptured
face of a Greek warrior. "And that of Pericles beside him, just
as I told you."

"Ha!" the second man exclaimed harshly. "You are right!
An act of gross impiety! An insult to the Goddess! Now, for
this offense we can attack not only Phidias, but Pericles him-

self. The proof is clear. To serve their petty vanity these two have made sport of Divine Athene! For that the law provides just punishment, nor can they hope to evade it against the anger of the people! Come! A complaint must be lodged at once!" Muttering, the two men hurried from the temple.

When they had gone, Alcamenes crept forward, examining the figures on the shield. There was no doubt about it; two of the faces in the battle scene were those of Pericles and Phidias. With fear in his heart Alcamenes ran out to the sunlit crest of the Acropolis. The workmen engaged in setting the new panel in place had completed their task and were now gathering up their ropes and ladders. With a nod to them, Alcamenes hastened down the long marble staircase. Whatever happened, Phidias must be warned.

He found the sculptor bent over his worktable, modeling a figure of the sea-god Poseidon for the temple's pediment.

"Master!" he cried. "You are in danger!" In a few swift words Alcamenes told what he had seen and overheard.

Phidias, staring at his slim, muscular hands, sighed.

"The wrong is mine," he muttered, "although none was intended. I placed the portraits there, both as a way of signing my work and of giving credit to the great leader who inspired it. No thought of impiety entered my mind. Yet I can see how the enemies of Pericles will magnify the affair in hope of turning the people against him."

"There is still time to escape!" Alcamenes burst out. "You could take ship for Egypt, for Crete. . . ."

"And so leave Pericles, who is guiltless in the matter, to bear the blame? No!" Phidias shook his graying head. "I alone am at fault and if brought to trial shall so tell the judges. Better for me to stay, to suffer for my act, than by cowardly flight to bring discredit upon our leader!"

"What of your work upon the temple?" Alcamenes groaned. "It will be stopped."

"So our enemies hope. Their rage is not against Pericles alone, but against all he has done and is trying to do in beau-tifying the city. Through me they hope to charge him with impiety, and so, having turned the people against him, over-throw our democratic State. That shall not be brought about by any act of mine. But even though I am placed behind bars, the work upon the Parthenon must go on." Rising, Phidias went to a cupboard in the wall and took from it several rolls of parchment. "Here are my sketches for the panels of the frieze. Many are still lacking. To you, Alcamenes"—he held out the rolls—"and to Agoracritis under you, I leave the completion of my work."

"Master," Alcamenes whispered. "The responsibility is too great."

"Not so. You have the talent—the genius. I am sure of that. You will also have my help and my advice. Even in prison you can still come to me with your problems. Take up the task with good courage, remembering that you are working not for art, for beauty alone, but for the right of free men to live, to create! Give no thought to me. I am but one. What must be fought for, preserved, is the spirit in which we have all labored, here in Athens—not sculptors alone, but poets, painters, dramatists, philosophers, students of the physical and political sciences—from Socrates to Polygnotus, from Anaxagoras to Euripides! The spirit of freedom and democracy, which Pericles has given to the world—that is more important than any or all our works. Through no fault of mine shall his enemies be permitted to destroy it!"

Alcamenes, staring into the Master's impassioned face, heard the tramp of men in the street outside, the thunder of knocks upon the door. Phidias, smiling, raised his head.

"They have come for me," he said, almost gaily. "Courage, lad! While I am away, see that work upon the Parthenon is not delayed!"

The trial of Phidias, on charges of impiety, was brief and unsatisfactory both to his friends and to his enemies. Disdaining to offer any defense, the famous sculptor confessed his fault at once. The portraits of himself and of Pericles upon the shield of Athene had been placed there, he said, entirely without the latter's knowledge. This at once relieved Pericles of any blame in the matter, much to the disgust of those who had brought the charges. And while, in the face of his open confession, the judges had no course but to condemn Phidias to a term in prison, the great bulk of the Athenian people, although they revered their august Goddess, felt that the sculptor had been less impious than vain.

Phidias himself took his sentence unprotestingly, declaring
to the court that he considered it just. Under the wise leadership of Pericles, he said, all men, whether rich or poor, obscure
or famous, were equal before the law, and since he, Phidias,
had offended that law he should accept the penalties like any
other citizen. When friends urged him to appeal to Pericles,
then away on a naval campaign against the Samians, he refused,
saying that to do so would be to act against the democratic
principles which governed the Athenian State. He wanted no
special privileges and would accept none. The enemies of
Pericles were furious. They found the spear they had aimed
at the great leader's breast turned aside by Phidias' loyalty and
integrity. Even their hope of embarrassing Pericles by stopping
work on the Parthenon came to nothing. Alcamenes, assisted
by Agoracritis and the other pupils of the Master, threw himself into the task with furious energy. Day after day, as long
as there was sufficient light, the carving of the panels for the
frieze went on. The young men were determined to have the
work done before Phidias was released from his cell.

From time to time Alcamenes took his sketches and clay
models to Phidias for approval. The Master gave it, smiling;
he had long recognized in the young sculptor from Lemnos an
outstanding genius, as many of his panels from the Parthenon
now preserved in the British Museum prove.

Slowly but surely the work on the great temple proceeded.
The rear pediment, depicting the birth of Athene, had been
finished by Phidias before his arrest, and most of the figures

for the front pediment as well. This represented the struggle between the Goddess and Poseidon for possession of Attica, and only the figure of the Sea-God was lacking. Alcamenes carved it from the Master's partially completed clay model; there remained but a few more panels of the great processional frieze to be done.

On the day that the last of these was finished and set in place, Alcamenes went with Agoracritis to take the Master this joyful news. Both were shocked by his appearance. A sudden illness, brought on by lack of sunshine . . . the dampness of his cell, had left him weak and trembling; he shook with a constant cough but his eyes still held their accustomed fire.

"So your work is done," he said cheerfully, "and with it, mine. Nor is the greater part of that work to be found at the Temple of Athene. If I have also shown the Athenians that here none can rise superior to the law, then I have gained a greater triumph than by carving a thousand statues. Tell Pericles, when he returns, that I have made this sacrifice on the altar of democracy."

Alcamenes, troubled, shook his head.

"Your genius is too rare, Master, your life too precious, to be sacrificed in any such way. The beauty of the Parthenon will stand to inspire men long after our State is forgotten."

Phidias laid a thin, trembling hand on the young sculptor's shoulder.

"You are wrong, my son," he said. "The Temple of Athene is but stone and mortar, and will perish with the centuries.

But the spirit of freedom that has made such beauty possible will live on forever, so long as men strive to create. The enemies of that freedom, by attacking Pericles, have sought to bring back tyranny; and they have failed. But they will try again and again. At times they may succeed. But always men will remember the age of truth and reason we have created here, and from that memory will take new heart for the fight during the long years to come. Remember, that without liberty there can be no real art, either of chisel or brush or pen. Not only the bodies, but the souls of men must be free. . . ." A spell of coughing checked the great sculptor's words.

"You are ill, Master, and should not be kept any longer in this dismal cell. I shall go to Pericles as soon as he returns to Athens, demanding that you be released. For the dedication of the temple. . . ."

"No." Phidias shook his head. "I am more free behind these bars, justifying the laws of the state, than I should be walking the streets in the knowledge that by special favor I had evaded them. Were Pericles to liberate me, his enemies could justly say that for the sake of a friend he had overridden the doctrines of equality on which the State is based. In such subtle ways is government by the people defeated, and the spirit of democracy overcome. I shall serve my sentence without fear or privilege, so that every citizen of Athens may say to himself, 'Even Phidias is not above the law.'"

Alcamenes and Agoracritis went away, determined in spite of the Master's refusals to effect his release for the opening and dedication of the Parthenon. In this, however, they failed. Before Pericles returned from his victorious campaign against the Samians, the great sculptor died in his cell. He had given his life for the sake of an ideal.

The Parthenon, although in ruins, still stands, to inspire men not alone with its majestic beauty, but with the spirit of free-dom in which such beauty could be attained. This was indeed a Golden Age—an age that saw democracy triumphant!

As the years went by, and Athens became complacent and rich, I saw to the north a dark cloud rise. Warlike tribes of Macedon, jealous of the wealth and prosperity of the Greek city-states, united for conquest under a strong and crafty King. Philip, father of Great Alexander, marched ever southward, tricking the Greeks with false promises, soothing their fear of invasion with clever lies.

Only one among the Athenians had wit to see through his web of treacheries, courage to tear the mask from his covetous face. Demosthenes the orator, thundering his warnings year after year, urged the Greek states to forget their petty quarrels and unite in defense of their liberties. But the men of Athens, thinking themselves safe behind their walls, would not listen until Philip and his armies were almost at their gates. One by one, using both fear and force, the Macedonian had overthrown the other Greek democracies; now only Athens and Thebes remained to face his might. At last, in response to Demosthenes' call, their brave but unprepared armies marched forth to meet the invader.

On the field of Chaeronea the battle was fought, Macedonian phalanx against the citizen-soldiers of Athens and the Theban Sacred Band—trained troops of a leader bent on conquest, against the army of democracy, fighting for justice, free-

dom of the individual, peace. The destiny of mankind for centuries to come was decided on that bloody field.

From my temple high upon the crest of the Acropolis I
watched the beaten forces of democracy straggle back, knowing
well that more than a battle had been lost on the plains of
Chaeronea. When Thebes and Athens fell, Greek democracy
fell with them. Henceforth, whatever outward forms of liberty
Greece was to enjoy, each citizen knew that in future his every
act and thought, even his life itself, depended upon the word
of one man—the King. He had become the People, the State,
the Law.

On that fatal Field, King Philip, drunk with the wine of
victory, danced in mad triumph upon the fallen bodies of his
foes, and Isocrates, greatest of Greek rhetoricians, condemned
himself to death by starvation, rather than survive with liberty
gone. After Chaeronea, Greece, under Alexander, had nothing
to give to the world but soldiers. Her art became the art of war.
The day of empire had dawned, and force, not reason, was
enthroned—the rule of the sword. Its first red fruits were murder—the murder of Philip himself, struck down by an assas-
sin's knife in the early days of his triumph.

For twelve years I watched his son, Great Alexander, march
up and down the world, winning many victories, pouring out
rivers of blood upon the altar of his self-esteem, seeking new
worlds to conquer. To please a courtesan he burned lovely Per-
sepolis; to gratify his vanity he had the priests of Egypt pro-
claim him a god. In an idle moment, to show his authority, he

slew his best friend. A million men died, that he might ride crowned with flowers through the streets of conquered Babylon. Soon he died as he had lived, in a blaze of drunken glory, and the empire he had carved with the sword fell apart like a fruit rotten to the core.

Yet it was not defeat at Chaeronea alone that sealed the fate of Greek democracy. The cankers of ease and prosperity had already begun to eat deep into the hearts of the people. In their pride and wealth they forgot that freedom is more than a word to be idly spoken, and liberty more than a temple set on a hill. It is also a way of life to be followed, a jewel to be jealously guarded, a lamp to be kept forever burning, lest the temple prove no more than an empty shell.

I stood at last before the matchless Parthenon, holding my torch aloft with none to see. Before me lay a dead city. Beauty remained, ships came and went in the harbor, men ate and drank and counted their gold, but Faith in my ways had departed from them; my temple was deserted; the people, no longer trusting democracy, dreamed of security instead.

But across the blue Ionian Sea, on the banks of the river Tiber, other men, stout of heart, had begun to follow my beacon light, men who marched beneath a standard that bore the gleaming letters S.P.Q.R.—the Senate and People of Rome.

AT THE RUBICON

THE midwinter evening was pleasant, although a trifle cool, and as usual when election time approached, the streets of Rome were filled with noisy and excited crowds. Soldiers, actors, sidewalk peddlers, gladiators, along with ordinary citizens, jostled one another from curb to curb. Gangs of the roughest elements, calling themselves political clubs, marched turbulently up and down, cheering for their favorites or engaging in violent street brawls with the supporters of rival candidates. Chosen for their fighting ability, thugs and bravoes plentifully supplied with money by unscrupulous leaders, headed these mobs.

Marcus Silius Albus, strolling along the Sacred Way, was particularly interested in the coming elections since now, for the first time, he could vote. Only the previous March, being then sixteen, had he ceased to wear a gold amulet case about his neck, put off the purple-edged toga of youth to don the all-white robes of a man. On that day he had seen his name entered in the books at the Record Office as a full-fledged Roman citizen, entitled to cast his ballot at meetings of the Comitia, the Popular Assembly, to elect tribunes and other public officials, ratify election of consuls, and approve the laws made by the Senate. Marcus belonged to a patrician family. His father, Sextus Silius Albus, was a senator and, like other senators, held office for life. But under the laws of the Republic, the acts of the Senate had to be approved by the people, as the letters S.P.Q.R. made clear. They stood for *Senatus Populus—Que Romanus*, The Senate and People of Rome, and formed the emblem of Roman democracy.

Marcus, having circled the foot of the Palatine Hill, was just entering the Appian Way when he heard a loud commotion ahead of him—men shouting, women screaming, and above their voices the sharp clash of arms. He pushed on, eager to discover the reason for all this excitement. On every hand he heard names being roared—"Clodius!" coming with leather-lunged violence from one group—"Milo!" from another.

To avoid being knocked down, Marcus backed to the edge of the road. At the center of the crowd he saw two men fighting with swords. The taller of the two drove his opponent back with fierce blows, daring him to stand and fight. Suddenly the shorter man slipped and fell to one knee. In an instant the blade of his adversary pierced his throat.

Horrified, Marcus saw the stricken man roll into the gutter, blood gushing from his wound. The victor, hastily sheathing his sword, made off, surrounded by his followers. Others, evidently adherents of the fallen man, bent over his body, but on discovering that he was beyond help, they also took to their heels. The crowd of spectators backed away, not wishing to become involved in the affair. A slender, lean-faced man was thrust almost into Marcus' arms. His carefully pressed toga, his richly decorated shoes, suggested a person of consequence—a patrician. For a moment he stared at the body in the street, then turned to Marcus.

"You saw the blow struck!" he said eagerly. "Can you name and bear witness against the one who struck it?"

"I cannot." Marcus shook his head. "Neither man was known to me."

The lean stranger glanced about. Through the darkness could be seen blazing torches as a file of soldiers issued swiftly from the Capena Gate. Excited citizens were guiding them toward the scene of conflict. The stranger grasped Marcus by the elbow, urged him into the shadows that clustered along the city wall. Walking swiftly, they came at length to a small wine shop.

"Inside!" the lean man said, "before any see us. This is an affair of great moment. There are questions I must ask." He pushed Marcus through the door of the shop, sank to a table and called for wine.

"Who was the man killed?" Marcus inquired.

"Publius Clodius, party manager for the Proconsul Gaius Julius Caesar, who, although in Gaul, is now the political master of Rome. Clodius was candidate for a praetorship."

"And the one who killed him?"

"Titus Annius Milo, the tribune, who is running for office as consul. A scurvy rascal if there ever was one!" The lean man's eyes were questioning. "How comes it you do not know these men, being a citizen of Rome?"

"For two years I have lived in Spain, sent there because of ill health. A long fever ——"

"Your name?"

"Marcus Silius Albus."

"Son of the Senator Sextus?"

"Yes. And you?"

"Quintus Cassius, a friend of Caesar's. With your help I mean to have this scoundrel Milo punished as he deserves."

"I see." Marcus took a sip of the sour wine a servant had brought. "Of what party is Milo?"

"The party of the Senate! The *optimates*! Rich and overbearing patricians who treat the people like dogs!"

"Then," Marcus said shrewdly, "in opposing Milo I should also be opposing my father."

"What of that? It is every man's duty, especially every young man's duty, to form his own opinions in times like these. You saw this Milo commit a shameful murder! As a good citizen you should wish to see justice done, and so help Caesar's cause."

Gangs of the roughest elements, calling themselves political clubs, engaged in violent street brawls.

"I know nothing of Caesar's cause nor of the man himself, save that in Gaul he has won many victories."

"Then I will tell you more. He is a friend of the people. If he fights the power of the rich and arrogant Senate, it is to restore to the plebs their ancient rights. Besides, he is a military genius, as all admit. Now that his second term of service as proconsul in Gaul draws to a close, he would return to Rome and seek due reward by election as consul of the Roman State. To that, I and all his many friends are pledged. It is his right."

"Yet," Marcus said, "I have heard him much spoken against."

"No doubt—by the patrician crowd. They envy him his power among the masses. That is why this scoundrel Milo murdered Clodius, to injure Caesar, whose supporter Clodius was. As a good Roman you cannot justify such criminal methods. What will become of the Republic if ruffians like Milo, acting on behalf of the Senate, thus strike down the friends of the common people? This dead Clodius controlled a great plebeian vote. How can the Senate and People of Rome govern jointly if the voice of the masses is not to be heard? Caesar is a champion of the *populares*, a champion of true democracy. He will not allow the will of the people to be ignored!"

Marcus nodded, greatly impressed.

"I would hear more of him, Quintus Cassius," he said.

Cassius emptied his wine cup and rose.

"Later, Marcus Silius," he replied. "Now I have much to do. This murder will set all Rome by the ears. I shall ask you to testify that you saw Milo strike the fatal blow. Come to my house tomorrow. It stands near the point where the Sacred Way turns toward the Forum. Anyone will direct you. I plan to have you meet other members of our party, young men like yourself who have the welfare of the Republic at heart. You are the ones to make Rome truly great. Friends of the people, who see that a new era is dawning. You must talk with Caesar's friends, with Marcus Antonius, with Decimus Brutus, with Balbus." He clapped Marcus on the shoulder. "Promise me to come. We need young men like you."

Flattered, Marcus gave his promise. At home he found his father getting ready for bed and told him of the murder he had witnessed on the Appian Way, but of his meeting with Quintus Cassius he said nothing.

A year and a half had passed since that exciting night, and the Senator Sextus Silius Albus sat at a table in his library, staring at a letter he had received earlier in the day. His toga, slightly open at the chest, disclosed, woven into his woolen tunic, the broad purple stripe which marked his rank.

The high-ceilinged room was lined with rows of pigeonholes, each holding many rolls of parchment and papyrus. The Senator was a great reader, especially of the classics. Copies of Plato's *Republic* and other works of the famous Greek philosophers lay on the table along with the letter he had just put down. The day was warm, but a pleasant breeze swept into the room through the open roof of a hallway adjoining.

The Senator looked up as Marcus entered. For a long moment he sat regarding his son sternly.

"You sent for me, sir?" Marcus began.

"Yes. Yes." Sextus tapped the letter he had been reading. "I have today heard from my old friend M. Tullius Cicero, who as you may know is now serving as Governor of Cilicia."

"I hope he is enjoying good health," Marcus said. He well remembered Cicero as the orator who had so ably defended Milo when the tribune had been tried for the murder of Publius Clodius. In spite of Cicero's eloquence, however, Milo had been declared guilty and sent into exile. Others beside Marcus had seen that fatal blow.

Sextus smoothed back his iron-gray hair. His expression was grave.

"Yes," he said. "His health is excellent. I have decided, Marcus, that your own would be improved by a journey to Cilicia. Perhaps a year spent under the tutelage of so able a man as Cicero might give you a better knowledge of the nature and purposes of our Roman Republic."

Marcus stared at his father, confused. He had been in excellent health ever since his return from Spain.

"I am quite well, sir," he said. "Why go to Cilicia to study under Cicero what I can learn with less trouble here in Rome?"

The Senator frowned.

"Not, I am afraid," he said bitterly, "from those misguided men with whom for the past eighteen months you have been associating."

"You mean Quintus Cassius and his friends?"

"I mean the political supporters of the Proconsul Gaius Julius Caesar. For a year and a half I have watched you, hoping their influence would do you no harm. It seems I was wrong. This man Caesar is a dangerous rabble-rouser! A vain and ambitious schemer who by shameful bribery has made himself the darling of the mob! An aristocrat who has deserted his own class to truckle to the base passions of the radicals! Cicero, once his friend, now despises him!"

Marcus flushed to the tips of his ears.

"Many think differently," he protested. "Among the people ——"

"The people do not think," Sextus said coldly. "They are ruled by their stomachs and their emotions; by the free corn doled out to them; by parades, contests of gladiators, circuses; by the gold which ambitious leaders, acting through such black-guards as Clodius, have showered upon them. It is common knowledge that Caesar owes his political advancement to the unlimited use of money. Crassus, his friend, lent him over a million drachmas for such base purposes."

Marcus, hearing his father's bitter words, stood for a moment too angry to speak. Under the influence of Quintus Cassius and other friends of Caesar, his admiration for the Proconsul had grown to hero worship.

"I think, sir," he said gravely, "that you do an injustice to a great man—and a great soldier. What if Caesar did employ as political jackal this ruffian Clodius? Was Milo, who served your party, any better? If Caesar has given the people corn and circuses, so have many others."

"By the thunderbolts of Jupiter!" Sextus Silius brought his fist down upon the table with such violence that the rolls of parchment were scattered to the floor. "Does that excuse him? You have been too long exposed to such false doctrines. Your mind has become poisoned. That is what comes of spending your time at street clubs and political meetings! Listening to demagogues in Caesar's pay! Consorting with radicals! Plebeians! Scum!"

"They may be scum," Marcus retorted, "but they are still Roman citizens with the right to vote ———"

"Especially when paid for it, as they will be paid, to elect your friends and Caesar's—Quintus Cassius and Marcus Antonius—to be tribunes of the people. He needs their support in his fight against the Senate." For a time Sextus sat silent, shaking his iron-gray head. "I am afraid, Marcus," he went on patiently, "that you do not understand the serious dangers by which the Republic is now confronted. In the past, the Senate and the People of Rome governed jointly, with age and wisdom on the one hand serving to check youth and inexperience on the other. But that was before the days of conquest. Now Rome has made herself master of new dominions in Greece, in Spain, in Syria, in Gaul. Proconsuls, sent to govern those rich and distant lands, have poured a flood of gold into our public coffers, not failing meanwhile to fill their own private pockets. With such vast stores of loot to prey upon, is it any wonder that those who seek to administer these provinces and gather their taxes should be willing to pay well for the privilege? Such men as Crassus, Pompey, Caesar, have debauched the people of Rome with huge bribes, merely to gain greater riches and power for themselves. Crassus, but lately slain by the Parthians, piled up such stores of wealth that he was nicknamed Midas. With his friends, Pompey and Caesar, he formed a triumvirate to govern and rule Rome. Not as honest men, through the Senate and the People, but as dictators, bribing and corrupting the common herd. Now Crassus is dead, but Pompey and Caesar still remain to quarrel over the spoils. Only by ridding the State of both can Rome remain a republic."

This was an aspect of the political situation new to Marcus, and one quite contrary to what he had been told.

"I had supposed, sir," he said, "that Pompey and Caesar were close friends and would stand together against any who might oppose them."

"No longer." The Senator gathered up his scattered parchments. "Pompey, as you know, was married to Caesar's daughter, Julia. Now that she is dead, their friendship wanes. Soon, I hope, we shall succeed in bringing Pompey to our side. Caesar, now approaching the end of his second term as proconsul in Gaul, must be deprived of power and his victorious legions, lest he do harm to the state. He is a vain but brilliant man, burning with ambition. With his work beyond the Alps ended, he now plans to return to Rome and seek election as consul. Were he to be given such honor, I predict that his first step would be to overthrow Pompey, so that instead of two consuls as provided by law, we should have but one. Next, he would force the Senate to name him dictator. That is why we of the Senatorial party oppose him. That is why we are working to bring Pompey to our side. We know Caesar's ambitions and do not trust him. I am telling you these things, Marcus, because since you have placed yourself among his followers your life may be in danger should Caesar attempt to oppose the Senate's decrees. Therefore, for your own good, I have decided to send you to Cilicia. Cicero is a man of good sense—a true supporter of our democratic form of government. Sit at his feet for a year, my son, and learn wisdom. If you remain here, if you continue to follow the fortunes of this adventurer, you will destroy yourself as he, if given the chance, would destroy the Roman Republic."

Sextus passed his hand wearily over his forehead. The effort of speaking at such great length had tired him. Marcus regarded his father without warmth.

"You say Caesar is ambitious," he replied, his voice grave. "That he is a man who seeks only to rule. Yet for many years he has served the State in Gaul so well that the Gallic tribes, instead of being a constant danger to the Republic, are now completely broken, without power to do us further harm. You say that if he is elected consul, Caesar would make himself dictator, yet what proof have we of that? I have talked with his friends, have read his letters, his dispatches, and find no such desire expressed. It seems to me he is a great and able leader whose purpose is to curb the power of the Senate, of the rich patricians who compose it, in order to serve the common man. He is champion of the people, of the younger generation, looking to a new era. Under his guidance, Rome will become stronger, greater than it has ever been before!"

Sextus Silius smiled—a grim, cold smile.

"You speak glibly, Marcus," he said, "in those rounded phrases of the demagogues. They have taught you well, these radical orators. Yet, I warn you!" The Senator's voice rose in sudden anger. "This man is consumed by a burning ambition. Under the false cloak of champion of the people he nurses a vanity that knows no bounds. Were we to give him the power, he would march his legions down the Sacred Way and trample our Republic in the dust—even seek, as did Alexander, to make himself a god!"

The two faced each other passionately.

"Will you go to Cilicia?" Sextus continued.

"No, sir, I cannot. My work, my future, lie here."

For a moment Sextus Silius fumbled with the parchments. His face might have been carved in granite. He spoke coldly.

"Then you must follow that future beyond my doors."

Marcus swept his toga aside, raised his arm.

"I am sorry, Father," he said. "Hail—and farewell!" In a moment he was gone.

Quintus Cassius, but recently elected tribune, sat in his garden, staring at the message he had just received.

"Caesar has crossed the Alps," he said, "and is now en-camped at Ravenna in the north."

Marcus, frowning, leaned forward on the marble bench.

"On his way to Rome and the consulship?" he asked.

Cassius shook his head.

"That remains to be seen," he went on frowning. "The regulations concerning those who seek public office are clear. No proconsul returning to Rome as a candidate for election may enter the State save as a private citizen. He must surrender his command, say farewell to his legions, before he can cross the Roman border. That is the law. So now he waits near Ravenna, which as you know is close to the frontier."

"But," Marcus objected, "why does he wait? Why not give up his proconsulship as the law requires?"

"Because, were he to return to Rome as a private citizen, he would be at the mercy of his enemies, of the Senate and of Pompey, who has now gone over to their side."

"Then what does he propose to do?"

"He hopes, by using his influence with the people's assembly, to have a regulation passed making it unnecessary for a can-didate seeking public office to come to Rome at all or even to make a personal campaign for office. Thus Caesar could remain safely at Ravenna with his legions while the vote is taken, electing him consul, in Rome."

"Do you think the Senate will agree?"

"They may, now that Caesar has offered to disband his army if Pompey will do the same. But Marcus Antonius is at the Senate Chamber now. We shall know more when he returns."

Cassius had scarcely finished speaking when the tribune came striding into the garden. His manner was agitated, his face flushed.

"Now by great Jupiter!" he cried, "the Senate has thrown off the mask! A decree has just been passed requiring that Caesar give up his office as proconsul, disband his army, before the first day of March or be declared an enemy of the State! Along with all who aid and support him!"

Quintus Cassius sprang to his feet, his lean, bony face twitching.

"That, my friends," he exclaimed angrily, staring at his two companions, "applies to us! If Caesar refuses to bow to the wishes of the Senate, our lives will be forfeit. As for myself, I am unwilling to take the risk! I leave for Ravenna at once!"

"And I as well!" Mark Antony added quickly. "We must carry Caesar the news, find out what he plans to do. And since I am informed that the roads from the city are being guarded so that leaders of his party may not leave Rome, I think we had best disguise ourselves as peasants and pass the gates on foot. Horses can be secured once we are safely beyond the walls." He turned to Marcus. "Provide yourself with money, my friend, if you plan to go with us. Don workman's clothes and return here within the hour. There is no time to lose!"

Marcus hurried away, his mind in a turmoil. He had not expected, when espousing the party of Caesar, that he would be forced to flee for his life. He understood better now why his father had wanted him to go to Cilicia. Still Caesar, he felt, was not only a very great leader, worthy of honest men's support, but a friend of the Republic, and would do nothing to injure its cause. This quarrel with the Senate must be smoothed out and the hero of Gaul given the consulship he deserved.

Since leaving his father's house Marcus had been living at the home of an elderly wine merchant who had charge of some property left him by his mother. Without explaining to anyone what his plans were, he secured a hundred drachmas, borrowed the worn tunic and cloak of one of the slaves, and hurried back to join his companions.

That night the three of them, having passed the gates of the city without difficulty, were galloping northward along the Flamian Way as fast as their horses could carry them.

The camp near Ravenna was not a large one since Caesar had brought with him only one legion—the Thirteenth—from Gaul. The rest of his army was following by easy stages.

The three horsemen, dusty and worn from their journey, splashed through the shallow waters of a frontier stream and rode up its farther bank. In the distance they could see the camp of the legion. As they came closer and passed by the sentries, they made out the figure of the Proconsul himself walking with Asinius Pollio and several of his trusted officers.

Marcus, as he and his companions climbed from their saddles, stood gazing curiously at the great soldier who had been victor during so many years of warfare in Gaul. He was a smallish, bald man of fifty with a keen, very intelligent face, but by no means the heroic figure one might have imagined. Holding the horses, Marcus remained in the background while Cassius and Antonius, hands raised in greeting, strode on.

"Hail!" Cassius said. "We bring bad news!"

Caesar welcomed his friends with a cool, thin smile.

"I have been expecting it," he replied calmly. "Pompey has declared for the Senate."

"Worse—much worse!" Cassius exclaimed. "You are given until March first to resign the proconsulship and disband your army."

"And if not?" Caesar asked.

"Then you and all your party are declared enemies of the Republic! We escaped, as you see, in the garb of peasants!" The tribune gazed angrily at his mean and dusty cloak.

Mark Antony, who had been silent until now, raised his head. He was a tall, strikingly handsome man, and even in his coarse woolen garments looked every inch a soldier.

"What are your commands, Caesar?" he asked bluntly. "We are here to carry them out."

"Let the men of the legion be drawn up. I will speak to them," the Proconsul said.

Marcus saw the encampment wake to sudden life. Trumpets sounded. The standards were brought forth, centurions sprang to the command of their hundreds. In an amazingly short time the four thousand men that made up the legion were ranged in the form of a three-sided square before the camp.

Facing them, Caesar began to speak. He had, Marcus noted with surprise, a fine, ringing voice, of greater volume than might have been expected from one of his slender physique.

"Soldiers of the Thirteenth Legion!" he said. "You have served me well beyond the Alps. You may have reason to serve me even better now. Although with your help I return victorious over our foes, my enemies in Rome, envious of my success, are determined to destroy me. For the victories I and you have won, my reward is a decree just passed by the Senate ordering that I resign my office as proconsul and disband my army by the first of March! Unless I do this, I and all who support me will become enemies of the State." He paused for a moment as deep rumblings of anger rose from the ranks of men.

"Such is the gratitude of republics!" he thundered, and swinging about, he pointed to the narrow waters of the Rubicon. "Beyond that stream lies Rome! If I cross its banks as a private citizen, seeking election as consul, my enemies will have me in their power. If I remain here, in command of an army, I shall break the law. What I decide to do depends upon your loyalty. Will you follow me in any course I may take? Soldiers of the Thirteenth Legion, I await your answer!"

He paused. Instantly came a roar of assent from four thousand throats. Marcus, thrilled, stood watching the scene, wondering which of the two courses Caesar would take—give up his command or, defying the Senate, keep it. There was a third course, however, which had taken shape in the Proconsul's ambitious mind. It was destined to change the history of the world.

While the troops were still protesting their loyalty, declaring they would follow him to the death, Caesar drew his sword, raising it above his head.

"Then follow me now!" he cried, and strode to the banks of the Rubicon. "The die is cast!" he muttered to Mark Antony as he passed. A moment later he was fording the narrow stream.

The soldiers, confused for an instant by this unexpected action, sprang after him. Soon they were forming their ranks on the opposite bank, on the soil of the Republic of Rome.

Quintus Cassius joined Marcus beside the horses. His lips were twitching, his sallow face was covered with sweat.

"War!" he cried out. "This means war! Against the Republic!"

Marcus could not speak. A thousand questions, doubts, crossed his mind. Caesar had not only retained command of his army, thus defying the will of the Senate, but in crossing the Rubicon he had invaded the Roman State.

Quintus Cassius, still shaken by what had occurred, was mounting his horse. He waved to Mark Antony to join them.

"We must follow whether we like it or not," he muttered, giving Marcus a troubled glance. "For us, as for Caesar, the die is cast!"

Silent, they rode southward in the direction of Rome.

Marcus, bound as he now was to the chariot of their leader, soon discovered the scope of that great man's intentions. By the end of the month Caesar was in Rome, forcing a terrified Senate to carry out his wishes. Then, having driven Pompey across the Adriatic into Greece, he proceeded to crush the armies of the Republic in North Africa and in Spain. This done, he followed Pompey into Thessaly and destroyed him utterly at the Battle of Pharsalus. A voyage to Egypt completed his conquest of that country through Cleopatra, its queen. Meanwhile, overriding all constitutional authority, he had himself named sole dictator for life. In less than four years, by the military might of his legions, he made himself absolute master of the Roman world. The Republic of Senate and People no longer existed. A crown, offered him by Mark Antony, he thrust disdainfully aside. Caesar was too great for such trifles as crowns. Like Alexander, he aimed at divinity.

Marcus, at last completely disillusioned, saw his hero's statue carried down the Sacred Way along with those of the other Roman deities. It was to be set up in the temple of Quirinius, with priests in attendance, and accorded divine worship under the name of "The Unconquerable God." It is not infrequently a delusion of Conquerors that, having made themselves masters of an earthly kingdom, they should aspire to the throne of Heaven.

Quintus Cassius, standing at Marcus's side, spat upon the flagstones.

"For this," he growled, "we have sacrificed our freedom! To make ourselves a god! But not," he went on angrily, "an unconquerable one! There are still men of courage in Rome!"

A few days later Marcus went to his father's house. Four years had passed since he had last entered it. He found Sextus Silius in the atrium, sipping a glass of wine. The Senator looked older, grayer. There were deep, troubled lines in his face.

Marcus ran forward, dropping to one knee.

"*Pater, peccavi!*" he murmured, grasping his father's hand. "I was wrong—utterly wrong! This man I thought a friend of the people served only himself! All that you predicted has come to pass! Forgive...."

"Yes." Sextus nodded. "You would have been wiser had you gone to Cilicia. My forgiveness is yours. I am glad that you have learned the truth even though too late." He glanced up as sounds of running footsteps, of men shouting, came from the street.

One of the servants appeared in the doorway, his face white.

"Master!" he chattered. "I bring terrible news. Mighty Caesar has been murdered! In the Forum! Stabbed to death by his friends at the foot of Pompey's statue! Mobs are carrying liberty poles through the streets, demanding that the rule of the Senate and the People be restored!"

Marcus sprang to his feet.

"Maybe it is not too late!" he said eagerly.

"Do not deceive yourself, my son." The aged Senator shook his head. "Caesar's nephew, Octavianus, will seize the reins of power, make himself Emperor. The Republic is ended! Greed and ambition have destroyed it! There will be no more liberty, no more democracy in Rome!"

In Rome I watched Caesar's nephew, young Octavian, swiftly and ruthlessly crush the last feeble efforts of the Senate and People to preserve constitutional democracy. Victor over his rivals by force of arms, he proclaimed himself Caesar Augustus, sole ruler of the mightiest empire the world had yet known.

Under the Caesars, Rome had law and order without liberty, justice without mercy, wealth and ease for a favored few and bondage for the masses. A servile and helpless Senate, appointed by the Emperor, merely echoed his decisions, and all under the purple lived and breathed by imperial favor alone.

From Britain to the Persian Gulf, from Spain to the Euphrates, Rome's iron legions marched, beating down her enemies, holding their peoples in slavery, pouring into her imperial coffers the looted wealth of the world. Calling themselves a master race, the Roman leaders forced millions to labor as beasts of burden throughout these conquered lands that a favored few at home might feast on ortolans and lamprey eels, washed down with snow-cooled wine. Frank and Gaul and Spaniard, Greek and Arab and Egyptian, Persian, Armenian and Jew, all bent the knee before the imperial eagles while a mad Caligula shocked even Rome itself by his excesses and a sadistic Nero tossed Christian victims to his tigers or laughed while the Eternal City burned. So far had men departed from the sane ways of democracy that they could grovel in the dust at the feet of half-witted Diocletian, proclaiming him a Heaven-born god!

Whatever in wealth and security Rome gave its citizens, it denied them man's most priceless possession—the freedom of his soul. Instead of dignity and peace under rulers of their own choosing, the Roman people were doomed to accept any ambitious tyrant who could seize the reins of power, as their government and their law. Like Alexander, the morally and intellectually bankrupt Caesars could vision only an empire based on military might, on force. They refused to listen when a greater authority than Rome warned that those who live by the sword shall perish by the sword. For five centuries after Julius Caesar crossed the Rubicon his successors lived by it. . . . Then I saw barbarians, refusing longer to endure in bondage, sweep down through the mountain passes to overrun Italy and hold even the Imperial City for ransom.

Blond and blue-eyed Northmen, blood-brothers of those who first carried my torch of liberty into Greece, men of a race who from earliest times had gathered in communal assemblies, in openly-held Things, to elect their chiefs and rulers. Despite Rome's conquering legions, the fires of freedom in their breasts had never ceased to burn. To them death in battle was better than abasement before some self-anointed king. As the power of Rome grew weaker and her imperial sword became dulled, these fierce warriors from the north advanced in ever-increasing numbers to topple the throne of the Caesars in the dust. At last only in the East where the city of Constantine stood did a Roman Emperor continue in power, ruling subjects of mixed Greek and oriental blood to whom freedom meant less than the perfumed pomp and luxury of an imperial court.

The love of liberty under law which had inspired the men of early Greece and Rome was, however, not dead. As Hun and Goth and Lombard swept over the Italian mainland, many refugees from the coast cities fled for safety to the islands of the great lagoon at the northern end of the Adriatic. Here they found hardy fishermen, descendants of the ancient tribes of the Venetii, who for centuries had dwelt upon these barren sand dunes, drawing their livelihood from the sea.

As the numbers of these refugees increased, they built towns and cities upon the many small islands that bordered the lagoon or dotted its broad and marshy surface. Soon their small fishing boats became great cargo ships, carrying on trade with all the ports of the Mediterranean.

High above the mud flats of these brave and hardy seafarers I raised my flaming torch of liberty. Beneath a banner bearing the Lion of St. Mark, the citizens of the Most Serene Republic of Venice traveled the pathway of democracy, led by elected rulers. Slowly, peacefully, they labored until their prosperity caught a Conqueror's eye. To Pepin, the Hunchback, son of mighty Charlemagne, these towns and cities of the lagoon seemed a fair and easy prize, from which great tribute might be wrung. With ships and men-at-arms he came to collect it.

I watched the struggle with a heavy heart, knowing the power of the Franks—knowing too that the new republic was unprepared for war. But miracles can sometimes be wrought when the spirit of patriotism burns high. In the hour of her danger Venice looked to the stars.

LOOK TO THE STARS

IN THEIR capital, Malamocco, a gray-walled city of the outer barrier, the Venetian people were desperately alarmed.

Rumors had begun to spread of an invasion from the Italian mainland by warlike Franks, eager to place the towns and cities of the island Republic under their rule.

A great war galley had been sighted that day, coming up the narrow channel that led from the Adriatic Sea into the quiet waters of the Lagoon, and a crowd soon gathered along the docks, wondering what this visit might portend. Although still far off, it could be seen that the vessel carried a broad white flag.

From the deck of his small fishing boat, Pietro Sapini watched the oncoming galley with curious eyes. Even at that distance he could tell from her build and rig that she was not a Venetian craft. As the vessel came closer, he knew this even more surely from the dress of the rowers at her benches, the weapons and armor of the fighting men gathered in a group at her bows. These men, he thought, must be Franks.

A tall, red-bearded warrior headed the group. His steel cap was circled by a band of yellow stones, and from beneath the edge of it ruddy hair fell in long twisted plaits. A tunic of linked mail reached halfway to his brawny knees; a fur-lined scarlet cloak hung from his shoulders. He carried a heavy sword at his left hip, and in his hand a bright steel ax.

As the galley came alongside the stone docks, Pietro sprang from the deck of his skiff to the shore. Like the rest of the crowd, he was eager to find out what these strange visitors wanted.

At the moment when the galley was first sighted, preparations to receive them had been begun. Already a group of dignitaries and officers of the State had assembled at one end of the wide cobble-paved piazza facing the waterfront. Here stood the *castello*, a handsome structure built of stone brought from the Italian shore.

On its broad portico the Doge, Obelario, sat in a gilded chair, surrounded by the elected tribunes from the twelve island townships that made up the Venetian Republic. The piazza was crowded but lines of soldiers armed with spears kept a way open through the throng. By dint of much pushing and squirming, Pietro managed to reach a point near the steps of the *castello*, from which he could hear and see all that went on.

About him the people were muttering and grumbling. The Doge Obelario was not popular with the citizens of Malamocco, because he had married a Frankish wife. Some even went so far as to hint that he was in the pay of the Emperor Charlemagne.

The crowd became silent as the fiery-bearded warrior strode forward between the two lines of spears, followed by his grim-faced bodyguard. Watching them, Pietro thought he had never before seen such brawny and powerful men.

The Franklish envoy, on reaching the steps of the portico, offered the Doge and his companions no greeting other than to raise his glittering ax.

"I bring to the rulers and people of Venice," he announced in a loud harsh voice, "a message from my liege lord, Pepin, son of mighty Charlemagne and by his grace now King of all Italy. Since it is known that you who dwell here in these islands and marshes came originally from his domains, and are thus his servants and vassals, I now call upon you to submit yourselves to his royal authority, acknowledging him as your rightful Lord and King!"

On hearing this insolent demand, a murmur of anger rose from the crowd. The Frankish warrior swept his audience with hard and scornful eyes.

"My Master, King Pepin," he went on, "is now at his city of Ravenna, awaiting your reply! Already his ships and his men have gone forth against your strongholds at Brondolo and at Chioggia! Unless hostages be sent within seven days, bearing tribute, your towns and cities will be taken by force, and all who resist put to the sword!"

Now the mutterings of the people became a defiant roar, and the Frankish warrior's bodyguard pressed closer about him, fingering the hilts of their swords. But the Doge, rising from his gilded chair, addressed the envoy softly, a faint smile upon his pale and crafty face.

"Tell your royal Master, O Chieftain of the Franks," he said, "that we will consider his message carefully and in due course, returning thereafter such answer as the government and people of our Most Supreme Republic shall deem best."

The envoy of King Pepin and his followers strode back to their ship, staring contemptuously at the angry and silent crowd. But when the galley had passed from sight down the channel, the people turned to the Doge, still standing at the steps of the *castello*.

Sensing their anger, he raised his hand. Pietro saw that it trembled.

"This is not a matter to be decided lightly," the Doge said. "We are in grave danger. I must take counsel with the tribunes and the officers of State. It may be that rather than see our cities attacked, our women and children slain, we should be wiser to pay tribute to this Frankish king."

"No! No!" came in furious roars from the people. "Let us fight!" Some, enraged, cried out "Coward! Traitor!" But others counseled caution, arguing that the overlordship of the young King, and of his mighty father, Charlemagne, might prove a shield against the Greeks at Constantinople, whose Emperor also sought to control the affairs of the island Republic. So the people disputed wordily among themselves, while the Doge and his officers retired to the council chamber of the *castello* to discuss the Frankish demands.

Pietro, now that the time for his evening meal was approaching, turned to go back to his boat. A party of citizens moving in the opposite direction stopped him. Several excited men were urging an aged and poorly dressed woman toward the marble fountain at the center of the square.

"Make way! Make way!" they shouted, pushing through the crowd. "Let the Poverina be heard!"

Pietro at once recognized the woman as an ancient and poverty-stricken crone who sold amulets and love philters to the youth of Malamocco, and who had some repute in the town as a prophetess, a weaver of mysteries and caster of spells. He waited to hear what she might have to say.

The men lifted her to the broad base of the fountain, from which she could overlook the crowd. Gray hair stood out about her seamed and wrinkled face like the quills of a porcupine; her eyes made Pietro think of hot coals. With a gesture of one bony arm she brought silence. The people, angered by the soft words of the Doge, were in a mood for defiance, and the Poverina was known to be an ardent patriot and republican.

"Men of Malamocco!" she began, in a high, shrill voice. "Citizens of Venice! Long ago when a child I was told at the knees of my grandsire how our island Republic began! How the people of the mainland, threatened by barbarians, went to their churches for aid! How at Altinum the good Bishop, seeing his flock in danger of death from these infidels, prayed to God for help. Then out of the sky came a great voice like thunder, bidding him mount his high tower, look to the stars! Now the heavens were clouded in darkness, but from that high place the Holy Man saw the lights in the huts of the fisherfolk, shining like stars over the deep waters of the lagoon. So, knowing that God had shown him this as a sign, the good Bishop led his people across the marshes to our islands—to Torcello, to Burano, to Mazzorbo! Let us also, in this hour of peril, look not in fear at the mud beneath our feet, but up, to God's stars!"

The people muttered approval, and the old woman went on.

"Do you not remember, my friends, what message our fathers sent to the Emperor of the Greeks, when the Exarch Longinus came here from Constantinople, asking our aid in their wars? Making threats, should we refuse? Think well, men of the Republic, what reply we sent! 'Tell your Emperor, O Longinus, that God, who is our help and protection, has saved us in order that we may dwell in peace upon these watery marshes! This Venice we have raised in the lagoons is a mighty habitation, where no power of Prince or Emperor can reach us save by the sea alone, and of them we have no fear!' So spoke our forefathers to the Emperor of the Greeks! Shall we do less, to this Frankish King?"

Now the crowd in the piazza broke into such violent and furious cheers that they were heard in the council chamber, and one of the tribunes, Angelo Badoer, from the islands of the Rialto, came out to learn the cause of the commotion.

"Down with the Doge!" the people cried, before he could speak. "No tribute to the Frankish dogs! Venice must remain free!" At last, however, the crowd became quiet, consenting to listen. Badoer addressed them.

"Men of Malamocco!" he said. "Your city is on the outer shore, and will thus be first exposed to the Frankish attack. I, as I need not tell you, come from Rialto, six miles away, near the center of the lagoon. The narrow channels across the marshes are unknown to our enemies, and may more easily be defended. Thus if I counsel resistance to the Franks, there may be some who will say that I leave you of the outer barriers to do the fighting, while my own people in Rialto are safe from harm."

The tribune paused, and many in the crowd murmured agreement, saying they would have to bear the brunt of the battle. Then Badoer raised his hand.

"Yet I *do* counsel resistance!" he shouted. "But were I in charge of the nation's affairs, I would, while stoutly defending ourselves with ships, order all who dwell in Malamocco and the other outer towns and villages to retire to Rialto, there to await the outcome of the struggle. Here is no place for the Republic's capital, exposed to the first onslaught of our foes. From the islands at the center of the lagoon, with God's help, no power can dislodge us! Let all the people be moved to safety in the boats. Such is my advice. There be some among the tribunes who side with me, but others side with the Doge, counseling surrender, so no agreement has yet been reached."

On hearing this, many of the leading citizens of Malamocco pushed forward, demanding that a vote of the people be asked, a Committee of Safety set up to replace the Doge and to take charge of the defense of the Republic. They crowded the portico, forced their way into the council chamber, with the tribune from Rialto at their head. Soldiers ordered to clear the people from the piazza joined with the noisy throngs in demanding resistance to the Franks.

Pietro, being hungry, decided to leave the affairs of the Republic to those of voting age. As he passed the fountain at the center of the square on his way back to his boat, he saw the Poverina sitting huddled at its base. The old woman seemed both weak and helpless, and Pietro, who had been deeply thrilled by her brave speech, stopped for a moment and touched her arm.

"You are tired, mother," he said. "Let me take you home."

She clung to him, trembling, but a flash of pride lit up her withered face and Pietro, seeing it, thought she must once have been very beautiful.

"Thank you, my son," she murmured. "I am glad that all have not forgotten me."

"None could," Pietro told her, "having heard your stirring words. Where shall I take you?"

The Poverina told him—a place on the outskirts of the city, where the salt workers had their homes. Salt, evaporated from sea water in great kettles, was one of the Republic's chief articles of trade.

Pietro set the old woman aboard his fishing craft, sculled it down one of the narrow channels cut through the mud flats, their banks held in place by twisted wattles that were fixed to rows of piles. Presently she pointed out a small, dilapidated hut near the edge of the canal.

"There is my dwelling place," she said. "Come ashore and I will give you some supper, such as I have, although you may fare better at home."

"This is my home," Pietro grinned, tying his boat to one of the piles. "Since my parents died I have had no other. And here is my supper." He drew from beneath the deck a covered basket. "Some fat eels, and a fine tuna fish that I held from my catch. There is also oil, for their frying, and a small jug of wine. Come . . . we will make a little feast, eh, mother?"

Soon the small bare room of the hut was filled with appetizing odors. Pietro, gazing about the place, understood why the old woman was called Poverina.

When they had eaten, she seemed stronger. A new fire shone in her eyes.

"My son," she said, "since you have no other home, promise to come here each night after you have sold your fish in the market. I can cook your evening meal for you and hear what news you may bring from the city. If these Frankish dogs come to Malamocco and our people flee to the isles of the lagoon, I have in mind a plan to save them from disaster." But what her

plan was, the Poverina would not say in spite of Pietro's ques'
tioning.

He went to bed early aboard his boat, and was out with his
nets before dawn. At high tide almost all the wide expanse of
the marsh was covered with water, but when the tide fell, many
channels were to be seen stretching through the mud, some
broad and deep, others very shallow. As the sun rose he could
see, far off to the west, the red-tiled roofs and shining towers
of Rialto. The main canals through the lagoon were marked
by stakes driven into the mud, but in his light fishing craft
Pietro could sail almost anywhere, especially at high tide.

By afternoon he was back at Malamocco, selling his catch to
the marketers. From them he learned, each day, the latest news,
carrying it back at evening to the Poverina.

Obelario, bowing to the demands of the people, had stepped
aside in favor of a Committee of Safety headed by Angelo
Badoer. The Tribune promptly gave orders to block the ap'
proaches to the city from the south and the east by sinking
hulks in the canals and stretching iron chains across them. At
the same time preparations went swiftly ahead to move the
people of the outer islands across the lagoon to Rialto. As soon
as this had been done, it was planned to pull up all the stakes
that marked the deep, main channels, thus making it difficult
for an enemy to penetrate the great marsh.

Day after day the flight of the people went on; and as news
of the Frankish advance came in, even small boats such as
Pietro's were pressed into service. Swift galleys from the south

brought word that King Pepin's warriors had overrun Brondolo and taken Chioggia; soon they were advancing along the
coast in the direction of Malamocco, both by water and by land.

The channel to the sea between Malamocco and the adjoining dune was not wide, and Angelo Badoer had a strong barricade—sunken hulks, the spars and masts of ships, driven into
the mud—built across it. Behind this barricade the Venetian
war galleys were assembled, ready to give battle should King
Pepin's ships break through. Badoer ordered it held at all costs,
until the people of the capital city had been taken to safety,
along with their household goods. Then the Venetian fleet,
with the fighting men aboard, was to retire to Rialto.

For many days the Venetians held the barricade, with the
Franks battling desperately to break it, but Venetian archers
on both ships and shore fought them off. Pietro, busy for
long hours each day ferrying refugees from the city to Rialto,
saw little of the fighting; but at night from the deck of his
boat he watched the lights of the Frankish war galleys and
heard the shouts of their men coming over the water.

At last all the people were gone, and Malamocco was a city
of the dead. That evening Pietro rowed very swiftly down the
narrow canal on which the Poverina's hut stood.

"Come quickly, mother!" he called to her. "Make a bundle
of whatever goods you would take. Tonight we sleep in Rialto."

The old woman stood at the door of the hut, shaking her
head.

"No," she muttered, as Pietro came up. "I stay here."

"But, don't you understand?" Pietro urged. "Our war galleys will leave during the night. When the Franks find out at dawn, they will be upon you! Make haste!"

The old crone did not move.

"I told you, my son," she said, "that when the Franks arrived I had a plan to save our people from disaster. That time has now come. Even yet I shall not tell you about it, but I call on you as a loyal citizen of the Republic to give me your help, obeying me in all things, whatever I command! If you will do this, swear upon the Blessed Cross. If not, go your ways, and I shall act as God permits me, alone!"

For a long moment Pietro looked into her burning eyes, then he touched the olivewood cross at her throat.

"I will obey you, Mother Poverina, in all things," he said, "and this I do solemnly swear."

"Good!" She regarded him, smiling. "Now bring in your basket that I may cook our evening meal."

That night Pietro did not sleep. Before dawn, loud shouts, the rattle of arms, the sound of trumpets, announced that the Franks beyond the barricade had discovered the retreat of the Venetians. Soon they were breaking down the barrier with axes, dragging the sunken hulks from the channel that their galleys might come into the lagoon. Meanwhile their fighting men swept through the deserted streets of the capital.

The Poverina appeared from her hut, leaning on a stout staff.

"Come, my son," she said. "Let us welcome King Pepin to Malamocco!"

Pietro sculled his craft along the winding canal until they came to the edge of the city. From here, by cobbled streets and lanes, they made their way to the piazza.

Bands of Frankish soldiers filled it, overflowing to the steps of the *castello*. Three mailed men seized them, asking what had become of the people of the city and where the Doge and his officers might be found. To all questions the Poverina refused any answers, saying she would speak only to King Pepin. At last, seeing that threats were useless, a chieftain ordered the two taken inside the *castello*.

Here, in the great council chamber, the Frankish King sat in the Doge's gilded chair, surrounded by his generals and courtiers. A slender, pallid man with a crooked back, his face wore a petulant frown. A heavy gold crown circled his helmet; his purple satin cloak was stiff with embroidery of precious stones and pearls. For a long time he sat staring angrily at the two prisoners; from his flushed cheeks and over-bright eyes, Pietro thought he must be suffering from a fever.

"What have we here?" he asked in ill-tempered tones. "I ask for the Doge of these islands and you bring me a ragged boy and a toothless crone! To what end?"

"They will speak only to you, sire," the chieftain said.

At this the Poverina nodded.

"I am a poor woman of Malamocco, O King of the Franks!" she said, in a high clear voice. "And with me is my son, a fisher boy, who earns our daily bread with his nets. The Doge and all the people have fled to certain islands in the lagoon known as the Rialto, which can be plainly seen across the water."

"Why did not you and your son go with them?" King Pepin asked sharply.

The old woman's eyes flashed like dark jewels.

"I am no friend of these purse-proud men of Malamocco, but a native of Heraclea, which city their Doge destroyed with fire and sword. For years I have dwelt in this place, a beggar. While others went in silks and fine linen, I starved! I stayed behind with my son when the people fled to tell you, King of the Franks, how you may overcome these men of Venice and so give me revenge!"

At this King Pepin's eyes glittered even more brightly but there was suspicion in them as he leaned forward in the Doge's chair.

"How?" he asked bluntly. "If you lie to me, old woman, I will have you torn apart by wild horses!"

"In this wise, O King," the Poverina went on. "Between here and Rialto runs a deep but crooked channel. By it, the Venetian galleys fled. But in their going they took up all the stakes and signposts marking the way through the marshes. Now you dare not venture across the lagoon in your warships, because your captains cannot tell what course to pursue."

"Ha!" The King sank back in his chair, snarling. "Well do I know that, fool!" he said. "Can you put back the stakes then? And if not, what have you to offer?"

"I have my son," the Poverina replied.

King Pepin stared at her stupidly, twisting his beard; there was a flicker of comprehension in his eyes.

"My son," the old woman went on, "who for many years has sailed the lagoon in all weathers, seeking fish for his nets. To him the secret ways of the marshes are open, even though the stakes be gone. By the color of the water, the shift of the tides, the position of the sun, the stars, he can guide your great ships to Rialto, going ahead in his small fishing craft. Thus you may come upon your enemies unawares!"

"Now by my soul!" the King exclaimed, "God has delivered these Venetian dogs into my hands!"

But one of his captains, standing nearby, shook a grizzled and doubtful head.

"How can we be certain, sire," he asked, "that in this channel the woman speaks of there is water enough for our ships?"

"There is enough," the Poverina said quickly, "but I have not told you all my plan. Here in Malamocco are many great barges, used by the builders to bring stone from the mainland. Let your fighting men be placed upon them. Let them be towed by the smaller galleys, which will be in no danger of going aground. Your larger vessels can then safely bring up the rear."

King Pepin straightened his crooked back and stared at Pietro sternly.

"Can you steer my ships in the proper channel, boy?" he demanded. "Without guideposts and stakes?"

Pietro did not look at the Poverina.

"Yes, sire!" he said.

A gray-bearded man at the King's elbow bent forward.

"I find no fault with the plan, sire," he muttered. "If we be sure these two speak in good faith, and are not traitors. . . ."

"What harm could they hope to do us?" Pepin asked, frowning. "Yet to make certain, let an archer be placed in the fisher boy's boat. The old woman shall accompany him. At the first sign of treachery, both he and his mother will be shot down." He turned impatiently to his captains. "Go, now, and look to the matter of the barges. If the old crone speaks truth, we shall take these islands of Rialto, and the Doge with it, before another dawn."

The mailed archer sat in the forepart of the skiff, his broad back resting against the mast. In one hand he held his short horn bow, an arrow notched to its string. The other lay at ease across his lap. In the fraction of a second he could raise his arm, let fly the dart.

Pietro stood at the stern of the skiff, driving it slowly ahead with twists of a long sculling oar. He possessed no weapons, other than the short steel knife at his belt that he used for cleaning fish. The old woman crouched silent at his feet.

Behind his light, shallow craft came a long line of galleys, each towing a barge crowded with fighting men. The heavier of the Frankish warships crept along cautiously some distance in the rear.

The afternoon sun was low, now, with the walls and towers of Rialto still over a mile away. The fleet of ships and barges

"Softly," Pietro frowned down at her. "The archer may hear."

had started early in the day, but they were heavily loaded and progress up the narrow, winding channel had been slow. Pietro, carefully examining each foot of the way, could not make use of his sail; had he attempted to raise it, he would soon have left that crawling fleet of barges far behind—and brought a quick arrow from the archer's bow.

The Poverina roused herself, touching Pietro's knee.

"Steer carefully now, my son," she whispered. "We are nearing the spot of which I sent word."

"Softly." Pietro frowned down at her. "The archer may hear."

"The fellow is Helvetian," the old woman said scornfully. "He does not understand our Latin tongue."

"Nevertheless, be careful. I know what I have to do." Pietro stared down at the water, watching with keen eyes its changing color. "Now I must turn," he went on under his breath, "but slowly, so that the shoaling of the water may not be observed." He gave the sculling oar a gentle twist. "From here the chan' nel grows shallower, as we move toward the north. Now that the tide is full over the marsh, even the larger galleys can pro' ceed, but soon it will begin to ebb swiftly, and then, Mother Poverina, some of those great ships will find themselves fast on the mud. So the way back will be blocked, and none of the smaller craft or the barges can escape from the trap. Then our swift galleys, knowing all the channels, will quickly destroy them." He gave the oar another twist. "Listen to me now, mother. When the archer raises his arm to draw back the arrow, throw yourself flat upon the deck; only so can you hope to escape. Then, before he has time to notch a second dart, I may with God's help be able to overcome him."

The old woman sighed.

"You are a brave lad," she whispered, "but I fear he will shoot first at you." Her eyes sought the towers of Rialto, red and gold in the dying light of the sun. The lines in her face, usually so deep-drawn, had suddenly vanished; she seemed to have found new serenity, new peace.

Far behind them faint, angry cries rose on the evening air, followed by the shrill call of trumpets. Pietro, glancing back over his shoulder, saw that one of the largest of the Frankish galleys had run aground. Straining at the oars, her crew tried to force her off the mud, but with the tide now rapidly ebbing, their efforts came to naught. The vessel ahead of her, also striking the edge of the marsh, swung around and crashed into the first one, thus blocking the narrow channel completely.

Hoarse commands came over the water, echoed from ship to ship. From the galley following the fishing skiff they reached the archer's ears. His arm swung up, the short bow bent. At the same moment the Poverina, instead of throwing herself upon the deck, sprang to her feet. Pietro was forced to step around her as he raced forward at top speed.

The bowman, his first arrow discharged, had already plucked another from his quiver. Before he could set it to the string, Pietro was upon him, buried the short, keen-bladed knife in his throat. As the man fell, the fisher boy hastily raised the skiff's small triangular sail. Only the wind could save them, with the first of the Frankish galleys so close behind.

The boat leaped forward. Turning back to the steering oar, Pietro gave a quick cry. The Poverina lay on the deck, a feathered arrow projecting from her breast. He knew, now, why she had stepped in front of him when that first dart was shot.

In a moment he was kneeling at her side. The stricken woman's face was calm and untroubled; she seemed to feel no pain. Tears gushed to Pietro's eyes.

"Mother . . . oh . . . mother!" he whispered, through choking sobs. He thought to draw the arrow from her breast but dared not, knowing that her life's blood would follow.

"How goes the battle?" she gasped.

Pietro glanced back. A cloud of Venetian war galleys had come from behind the Isle of Olivolo and was sweeping down upon the Frankish fleet, riding the swift ebb tide. Their pilots knew every twist and turn of the channels; the Franks, unable either to advance or retreat, lay at their mercy.

"The fleet from Olivolo has come, Mother," he said. "The enemy is thrown into confusion."

"Lift me up!" The old woman's eyes blazed. "I would see."

Pietro put his arm about her shoulders, raising her gray head. The sun had set, but in the afterglow the surface of the lagoon was like polished brass, with the masts and hulls of the ships etched in black upon it.

The swift and skilfully handled galleys of the Venetians attacked the crowded barges, splitting some in two, driving others upon the mud flats. In a few minutes the water was filled with dead and drowning men. So many perished in that bitter struggle that even now the canal at that point is called the "Channel of the Orphans."

"The Franks are beaten!" Pietro cried. "See—their barges are destroyed! Now our men are attacking the great galleys! I think that few of King Pepin's warriors will return to bring him the news!"

Soon the afterglow faded and darkness came over the wide sweep of the lagoon. Except for a few masthead lanterns, there was nothing to be seen; but through the gathering mists came faint cries of triumph, signaling a Venetian victory.

The Poverina sank back upon the deck.

"The Republic is safe . . . safe," she whispered, smiling. "Never forget, my son, what was told our people long ago." Her eyes sought the deep blue dome of the heavens. "Trust in God . . . and look to the stars . . . always look to the stars!"

The old woman's voice became still. Pietro, sobbing, knew that she would speak no more. He picked up the steering oar and turned his boat toward Rialto.

Over the shadowy mass of the islands rose the arch of the sky, a purple canopy, pierced by a myriad points of light. Far off he could hear the victorious Venetian trumpets. At his side the Poverina still seemed to hear them as she looked steadfastly up at the stars.

Not in Venice alone did the freedom-loving people of Italy turn to democratic forms of government. Elsewhere on the ruins of Imperial Rome I saw new Republics rise, ruled by assemblies and leaders responsible to their citizens. After centuries under the bitter domination of the sword, common men turned to more worth-while pursuits, more cheerful tasks than the shedding of blood to gratify the personal ambitions of vain and power-mad dictators.

At Genoa, great maritime port of the Tyrrhenian, another strong democracy came into being, led by men of the sea. Soon the heavily laden galleys of the Genoese Republic were carrying its commerce and its flag to all the cities about the Mediterranean, rivaling the fleets of Venice itself. Yet that rivalry was in the end to bring these two great sea powers into deadly conflict, so that through greed and love of power the strength of both was broken, their lifeblood sapped. When democracies turn to conquest, and free men take up the sword against their neighbors, they attack the very principles upon which their own existence and safety is based.

At Florence, that rare city on the banks of the Arno, I saw a new republic set up by the voice of its people. Here, in an atmosphere of peace and freedom, men of genius began once more to create beauty, undisturbed by the threat of the sword. Great works of art and letters were given to the world as they had been given in Greece fifteen centuries before, so that men spoke of a rebirth, a Renaissance, calling Florence another Athens. Sculptors and painters, poets and writers, craftsmen in gold and silver and the potter's arts flourished as they had never flourished under the iron rule of the Caesars; I saw such masters as Leonardo da Vinci and Raphael, Michelangelo and Benvenuto Cellini, give their immortal talents to enrich mankind. Yet Florence, like the other free cities of Italy, was doomed in the end to perish through lust of conquest and internecine war.

Far to the north, where Caesar's legions once built their camps, I saw the men of England, stiff-necked and proud, rise to curb the power of a Norman King. Feudal lords and barons, jealous of their ancient privileges and rights, demanding a new charter of liberty on the plain of Runnymead.

THE KING COMES TO RUNNYMEAD

GILBERT HERNDON, stepping from the tent that fresh June morning, smiled as he pushed the tangled mop of chestnut hair out of his eyes.

The duties of a clerk in Chancery gave him few opportunities to get away from London, to breathe the fragrance of budding trees and flowers and of the new-mown grass. His days were spent in musty law courts, filling countless sheets of parchment with dull records in smooth-flowing Latin or the more rugged characters of Norman-English script.

It was early, with the sun just up, and dew still covered the broad surface of the Running Mead in silvery, lacelike patches. The young grass was soft beneath his bare feet, but a chill in the air caused him to wrap his woolen robe closer as he ran down to the banks of the Thames.

On every side the wide green meadow was covered with tents, sheltering not only the great lords and barons, but their knights, squires and serving men. Banners bearing the arms of many noble English houses fluttered before the larger pavilions; their gay and brilliant colors made Gilbert think of a huge flower garden.

He stood for a moment shivering on the tree-lined bank of the river. Except for a few sleepy servants, scarcely anyone in the great camp was about. Far away to the north he could make out the tall, central tower of Windsor Castle, just visible through the mist. Now that lionhearted King Richard was dead of an arrow in France, his brother, dark John, slept beneath the royal standard at Windsor, ruling England evilly, so thought the many of his subjects gathered here upon the Mead.

Gilbert threw off his robe and plunged into the quiet river. The water seemed astonishingly cool for June. He swam about vigorously, his eyes on the sleeping encampment. These free men of England had come together, bound by a solemn oath to fight until death itself, in defense of their ancient liberties. One by one, it seemed to them, the King had usurped the rights granted Englishmen by previous charters; now the nobles of the realm had refused him both money and service until those rights were restored.

That, Gilbert knew, meant a busy day for him, since if the lords and barons, meeting the King, were able to force new promises from him, those promises would have to be set down in black and white on stout parchment and duly sealed, before any would trust the King's oft-broken word.

Shivering, Gilbert climbed up the bank, put on his thick woolen robe. As he hurried back to the tent he wondered how long the written document would be, and how many copies of it he and the other clerk brought down from London would be expected to make. Not every penman, he thought, could write such a smooth, round hand as his. Fewer still could work so swiftly. And when it came to using good Latin, scarcely any at all, outside the churches and the law courts. Even his fellow clerk from the Chancery, Timothy Smollett, was not his equal in this respect. As for Brother Anselm, the white-haired monk from the Abbey, he had not the strength in his fragile fingers to drive a quill pen hour after hour over the stout parchment for all he was a scholar. Such work required both a strong wrist and a cool head, to make sure that each letter was properly formed, each word correctly spelled, each line kept true and fair across the page. Also there were capitals and punctuation marks to be watched, omissions to be guarded against, and as for blots—they must be avoided as the Devil would avoid holy water, lest an entire sheet be spoiled and have to be done over.

The cooks and scullions of the camp were busy now around their fires, preparing breakfast for their masters. Gilbert thought it must be pleasant to lie abed while others toiled. But since he and Brother Anselm and fat Master Smollett were neither knights nor barons, but only common men, they must needs provide their own morning meal.

They were already up and about it when Gilbert got back to the tent. He put on hose and shoes, breeches and doublet and hastened to join them. Brother Anselm, kind and gentle, he liked, but Timothy was inclined to be sly and ill-tempered.

Soon the mess of fried mullets was ready, with bread and cheese, and cups of fresh milk brought in by the farmers. As the three ate, Brother Anselm discoursed in his soft voice.

"King John," he said, "has been guilty of grievous wrongs, not against the lords and clergy alone, but also against the people. In the days of good King Henry, the free men of England were assured that in return for loyal service they would be safe under the law in their persons, their property, and their lives. These things the King has taken away from them. Now the great lords and barons, in refusing fealty until these rights have been restored, speak not only for themselves, but for all the people from whom their strength and sustenance is derived. Here in England we have no place for tyrants, but only for those who govern justly with our full consent. Unless the King do so, he must be forced to it, or else thrust aside to make room for one who will. Such is our ancient custom."

Timothy Smollett's broad, heavy face twisted into a scowl.

"And what has King John done," he asked, "that his subjects should so turn against him?"

"That you will learn, my son," Brother Anselm replied, "when the list of the barons' complaints, and the remedies therefore, are placed before us. And since young Gilbert is swifter with the pen than you, Timothy, his shall be the task to set these matters down, while I read aloud the words to be written. Your part will be to compare what he has done with the rough screeds supplied to us, seeing that no words have been omitted nor any errors made. So we shall proceed swiftly."

"And do you think," Timothy asked, "that so great a task can be completed in one day? I am told that the King will be asked to sign a new charter."

"That is true." Brother Anselm set down his empty cup. "Such a charter can be prepared only after much discussion. But I am informed that this morning, as soon as the King arrives, a list of articles is to be presented to him, setting forth the barons' grievances and their just demands. These having been agreed upon, a fair copy must be prepared for the King to sign. Then the several articles can be discussed in detail, and the great charter written out. Our task today will be to prepare this list swiftly that the King may not be kept waiting nor the progress of the meeting delayed. The charter itself will come later, and of that several copies must of necessity be made." Brother Anselm went to the door of the tent, glancing out. "Now I see that carpets are being spread before the royal pavilion and a great chair set on the greensward. There will be no work for you, young men, until after His Majesty arrives. So go you forth and see what you may, while I prepare the table with pen, ink and parchment for your labors." He removed the platters from the broad oak board, sweeping it clear of crumbs. "But since your presence may soon be needed, do not stay away overlong."

Gilbert and Timothy left the tent. In the camp of the barons great excitement prevailed. Trumpets sounded; there was a clatter of arms and a neighing of horses as the knights, squires and men-at-arms gathered under their respective banners. What with the polished steel, fluttering flags, and rich robes of satin and velvet and cloth of gold, the broad green meadow presented a brilliant scene.

Timothy, dour and silent, marched off alone. Gilbert crossed the mead in the direction of the road which bordered it. Here, beyond the limits of the encampment, crowds of sightseers waited, to catch a glimpse of the King as he arrived from Windsor town. Few of these plain folk favored John; his brave-hearted brother Richard had been their *beau ideal*. But curiosity brought many scores from shop and field to gape at royalty and witness the stir of armed men within the camp.

Gilbert, arriving at the road's edge, heard approaching hoof-beats and the blare of trumpets. Through a thick cloud of dust a cavalcade of armored horsemen swept toward him. So swiftly did they approach that a small boy, darting into the roadway to recover his strayed sheepdog, stood in confusion, neither realizing his imminent danger, nor understanding the shrill cries of the onlooking crowd.

With no thought of the risk, Gilbert sprang to the boy's aid. Sweeping the youngster up in his arms, he dove headlong across the roadway under the hooves of the oncoming horses.

For a moment it seemed to the spectators that he could not escape; then, leaping clear, he plunged to his knees at the road-side, still clutching the frightened boy in his arms.

The crowd drew back to give him room, but seeing that the lad was safe, quickly turned its attention to the passing cavalcade. Behind those thundering horsemen, amid a forest of pennoned lances, rode the King.

As Gilbert raised the boy to his feet a white-faced girl ran up.

"Oh, sir!" she gasped, kneeling at the youngster's side, "I—I do thank you!" She had no eyes for the King's passing, nor seemed aware of it; her whole thought was for the youngster. "Tom, you foolish boy!" she murmured, breathless.

In spite of the girl's pallor and her obvious fright, Gilbert thought her very pretty.

"He's my nephew!" she explained, glancing up. "I brought him to see the knights and men-at-arms and the camp." Notic-ing that Gilbert was feeling his wrist she hurried on. "Oh, sir, I—I hope you have not hurt yourself!"

"A little," Gilbert admitted uneasily. Now that the King had arrived he knew he must hurry back to the tent. "I—I can not stop. . . ."

"But surely," the girl protested, "you will wait a moment until my father comes." Her eyes were no longer terrified; her cheeks had regained their color. "He is putting up the pony and cart, and will wish to thank you. . . ."

Gilbert's eyes were the ones to show terror, now. In falling he had put out his right hand to save the boy from shock.

"Oh, sir, I hope you have not hurt yourself." "A little," Gilbert admitted uneasily.

Mounting pain in both wrist and arm made him wonder if he could wield a pen.

The girl was smiling at him, her fingers caressing the young-ster's bright hair.

"My father's name is Page, sir," she went on. "William Page. And he is Head Forester at Windsor Castle. I am Margaret. . . ." She hesitated, flushing, as she saw Gilbert's frown. "Forgive me if I seem forward, sir. I would not seek to keep you, against your will ——"

"It isn't that." Gilbert's hand felt as if he held a fistful of hot coals. "I have work to do. Perhaps I could see you and your father another time. My name is Gilbert Herndon."

"You will be welcome, sir," the girl said, smiling. "We live in the lodge, close by the Great Park gate."

"I'll come," Gilbert said. "This evening, it may be," he added ruefully, staring at his rapidly swelling wrist. Not much chance of work keeping him, if he were unable to use a quill. "A good day to you, Mistress Page." He crossed the road and hurried back to the tent, wondering what he could say to Brother Anselm.

The aged monk stood beside the table. On it he had arranged inkhorn, newly sharpened pens, a sheet of parchment as long as a man's forearm. His pale, bright eyes dropped to Gilbert's dusty sleeve, his red and swollen hand.

"You have hurt yourself, my son?" he asked, frowning.

"Yes. I—I fell. . . ."

"On this, of all days!" Brother Anselm's frown grew dark.

"I am sorry. It could not be helped. A small boy ——"

The monk brushed aside Gilbert's explanations with a gesture, turning to Timothy Smollett, who now entered the tent.

"You will take Gilbert's place today! He has been skylark-
ing and injured his wrist. Perhaps, when the work is done, he
may be able to compare it, to see that no mistakes have been
made." There was cold anger in the old monk's voice.

Timothy grinned. Gilbert's accident caused him no regrets.

"The King has just accepted the demands of the nobles,"
he exclaimed. "When a list of them was read he glanced for a
moment at the great force his enemies had drawn up, and gave
a savage nod, muttered a quick oath. It was easy to see that he
was bitterly angered, but there was naught else he could do.
My Lord Pembroke and Stephen Langton, the Pope's delegate,
suggested some small changes and to these both sides agreed,
marking them on the rough draft. I think that in a few moments a messenger will arrive with it." Smiling complacently,
Master Smollett sat down at the table, turned back his sleeves
and selected a pen. "Well, I am ready, although I deem it a
shame for these over-proud nobles to set their wishes against
the will of the King. Indeed, I hold them foul rebels!"

At that Brother Anselm growled something in his throat, his
deep-set eyes fixed angrily upon Master Smollett's broad back.

"Hold your loose tongue, lad!" he said, "lest evil come upon
you! I, too, am such a rebel, ready to defend the liberties of
our people with my life! And so say all true Englishmen. We
want no traitors here!"

"You would defy the King's power, then?"

"Not his power, so much as the wrongful use of it. When the demands are written, you will see."

Then a young squire came to the door of the tent, a roll of parchment in his hands. He gave it to Brother Anselm.

"You are commanded, Sir Monk," he said, "to prepare as quickly as may be a fair and true copy of what is written here, ready for the King's seal. His Majesty waits in evil temper. Make haste, lest by delay his mind be changed."

Brother Anselm unwound the roll.

"The task shall be completed with all speed," he said, and the messenger left the tent.

Gilbert, despite the sharp pain in his wrist, listened with keen interest as Brother Anselm read aloud the flowing Latin words.

"Head it," he said to Timothy Smollett, " 'These are the Particulars of what the Barons ask and our Lord the King grants.' "

Slowly, carefully, in small, fine script, Master Smollett inscribed the brief heading across the top of his parchment page. Then, as the old monk continued to read, he went on with the body of the document.

There were forty-nine articles in all, and the work of setting them down progressed slowly. Standing at Brother Anselm's side, Gilbert read the list over his shoulder, checking each word as Timothy set it down. After a time, when the monk's voice grew tired, Gilbert read aloud in his stead.

Some of the articles, having to do chiefly with the nobles, their fees to the crown and their estates, did not interest him much; others caused his heart to swell with pride. One pro-vided that no free man might any longer be seized or im-prisoned except by due process of law, nor might he be tried save by a jury of his peers. All from high to low were made safe in life, liberty and property, and could not be deprived of them arbitrarily, even by the King himself. The church was to be free; limits were to be fixed to the power of those who levied taxes; there was to be strict regulation of the law courts, the duties and powers of bailiffs and constables, of weights and measures, of the rights to hunt and fish. Gilbert, who during his service of the law had seen hundreds of honest men robbed in various crafty ways, thrown into gaol without reason, denied justice unless they paid for it, cheated, plundered, wrongfully condemned—Gilbert gave a sigh of relief. If such bitter evils could be done away with, and the liberties of free men guar-anteed by charter under the great seal of the King, then a new day had dawned in England—not for the lords and barons alone, but for all the people!

At noon Timothy threw down his pen, grumbling that he was hungry and must eat. While he and Brother Anselm munched bread and cheese, drank pots of bitter ale, Gilbert compared what had been written with the rough screed and discovered a few minor errors. It shamed him to think that he had not done his part, but he was consoled by the thought of the small boy whose life he had saved and by visions of Mis-

tress Page's smiling lips and deep blue eyes. He would go to
see her, he decided, that very night.

At one of the clock Master Smollett, having eaten and
rested, again took up his pen, and by three the long page was
completed, with ample space at the bottom for the King's
seal. Brother Anselm himself, after Gilbert had compared the
remainder of the document, hurried off with it to the pavilion
in which King John and the leaders of the barons sat discussing
in detail the wording of the clauses that were to make up the
Great Charter.

From the door of the tent Gilbert could just make out the
King, sitting chin on hand in a black rage, while Stephen Langton once more read the List of Articles aloud, to assure all
present that no mistakes or omissions had been made. Then,
amidst a buzz of excitement, the royal seal was affixed.

Brother Anselm returned to the tent, smiling.

"Now that is done," he said. "We can do no more until
the Charter itself is ready for copying. This may not be until
late this evening. They will work at it as long as the light
holds, and even far into the night if need be. But we can not
begin our task of engrossing before the morrow, and since four
true copies are to be made, I have asked that three more clerks
be sent down from London." He glanced sharply at Gilbert.
"You, young man, will be of no use to us, for I can see that
your wrist is now swollen to twice its natural size."

"True," Gilbert admitted. "But I may be of service in com-
paring the copies, as before." He took from the table the roll

of parchment from which the List of Articles had been prepared. "What is to be done with this?" He held up the long
strip of vellum, covered by closely written lines, with many
changes and corrections scrawled in between them.

Brother Anselm glanced idly at the crisscrossed and unsightly
sheet.

"It is of no value," he said, "unless by scrubbing with water
and sharp sand the parchment is cleansed of what is writ upon
it. A difficult matter, for the ink soaks deep into the skin."

"Give it to me," Gilbert said quickly. "I have sometimes, in
the law courts, cleaned such pages in the past, and used them
for . . . for writing verses. . . ." He paused, coloring a little
under Timothy Smollett's loud laughter.

"Take it," Brother Anselm nodded. "As a reward for injur-
ing your wrist." His manner was grim. Gilbert thrust the roll
of parchment inside his doublet.

When supper had been eaten, and the platters washed, he
decided to pay his respects to Mistress Page and her father. It
was still broad daylight and at this midsummer season would
continue so for some time. It would be pleasanter, he thought,
to take a stroll than to sit for hours enduring Brother Anselm's
reproaches or Timothy Smollett's sly laughter.

As he left the tent, the light of candles in the royal pavilion
showed that the King and his advisors were still at work, preparing the final wording of the Great Charter.

He went along the road toward Old Windsor, and by dint
of inquiring came without difficulty to the gateway of the

Great Park. A small stone and timber lodge beneath the trees showed a light at one of its windows, dispersing the shadows of the huge oaks and elms.

A tall, stalwart man, dressed in a leather coat and carrying a hunter's knife at his belt, opened the door in response to Gilbert's knocks. On learning the latter's name he announced himself as William Page, and thanked the young clerk warmly for saving his grandson's life. Then Margaret Page, hearing their voices, ran down the narrow hall.

"It—it was good of you to come," she stammered, blushing. "Shall we sit for a while in the garden? There is a bench under the oaks, and the night is fine." She led Gilbert to a broad settle just inside the lodge gates, screened by a cluster of lilac bushes. "How is your arm? I was afeard you might be badly hurt."

"Merely a trifle," Gilbert laughed. With this sweet-faced girl beside him, and the perfume of lilacs in the air, he almost forgot the pain at his wrist. He drew his hand from inside his doublet, holding it up. "I am a clerk who can no longer use a pen, which is as bad as a soldier unable to wield his sword. Now others write the Magna Carta, while I sit in idleness, looking on."

"Oh." The girl seemed distressed. "I am truly sorry. Even though my father serves King John, he hopes, as all good men of England must, that the people will win back their rights. Tell me somewhat of this Great Charter the barons have asked."

Gilbert was surprised that so young a girl should be interested in such matters, but he described the demands the List of
Articles had contained in detail. She listened eagerly, nodding
from time to time in agreement.

"My brother Tom, who is the boy's father," she said, "is a
lay student and novice in the abbey at Westminster. He has
told me much of England's history, and of the long fight her
people have made to preserve their liberties, even against kings.
He, like my father, favors the barons' party, as indeed most
churchmen do throughout the land."

Gilbert, about to speak, checked himself as the sound of
hoofbeats came through the darkness and two men rode up to
the lodge gates from the direction of Windsor Castle. One was
a noble, wrapped in a rich, sable-edged cloak; the other a
knight wearing linked mail. They sat their horses just inside
the forest gateway, as though waiting for someone to arrive
along the road. Carrying a lantern the Head Forester came out
to question them. The noble replied harshly.

"We expect a messenger from the camp at Runnymead!"
he said. "Admit him, my man, without delay!"

Gilbert and Margaret Page sat silent and unseen behind the
lilacs. The two horsemen conversed, not knowing they were
overheard.

"I tell you, Geoffrey," the one in the furred mantle exclaimed, "the King will give us his blessing for this. He has no
desire to grant a charter to these pestilent rebels! Only yesterday he had news of fresh forces arriving from France. Granted

but a short delay and he can defy the barons and all their works."

"But today word came, Sir Hugh, that he had agreed to their list of demands."

"Only because he was forced to it by the power of numbers! He still seeks time and a way of escape! That we shall furnish him!"

"How?"

"This fellow we now await—a loyal clerk by the name of Smollett—hath a plan. What it is, I know not. When he comes we will take him to the King's small hunting lodge in the forest, and there hear what he has to say. Ho! I see someone advancing along the road. Keep quiet, Geoffrey, and leave the affair to me."

With the girl's shoulder trembling against his, Gilbert watched the stout figure of Timothy Smollett pass the forest gate. After a few whispered words with the two horsemen he disappeared among the trees, walking between their reined-in steeds.

"Who is that man?" Margaret asked. "Do you know him?"

"Yes." Gilbert got up. "A scurvy traitor from the camp. Can you lead me, quickly, to the King's hunting lodge? We must hear what these plotters have in mind."

Margaret nodded, grasping his hand.

"Come!" She began to run, softly but swiftly, along dark forest paths, curving in and out among the great trees, until they reached at last a low, timbered cottage perched at the edge of a small stream. Near its door two horses were tethered, stamping the soft earth. Cautiously, like a graceful fawn, the girl led Gilbert to the rear of the lodge, where a lighted window showed. Crouching beneath the lattice, they could hear the three men talking inside.

"You say, fellow," a stern voice asked, "that the old monk is alone in the tent? And will so be during the night?"

"Yes, Your Grace," came in Timothy Smollett's crafty tones. "Save for myself and a stupid lout with a sprained and helpless arm."

"What does that profit us?"

"An hour ago, when I left the camp, a roll of parchment was sent to the tent, on which was roughly inscribed the wording of the new Charter. Tomorrow, I, with other clerks coming from London, will begin the task of engrossing fair copies for the King's seal. Once these are prepared, and His Majesty, with the forces of the barons facing him, must needs sign. But should the copies *not* be ready, and the signing so delayed, then the King can retire in anger to Windsor, call for another meeting a week or two weeks hence. By that time his army will be assembled ——"

"Now by The Cross!" the older of the two horsemen cried. "The plan hath merit. But how is the preparing of the Charter to be delayed?"

"By stealing the rough draft the barons have made ready to be copied. Since no other exists, all the work of the meeting would then have to be done over again. Surely the King could justly fly into a rage, claiming his time and labor had been wasted."

"Without doubt." The older man chuckled. "So the only draft is in this aged monk's tent?"

"Yes, Your Grace. With my own eyes I saw him place it under his pillow. Send stout thieves, to steal the parch-ment ———"

"But," a younger voice objected, "this camp of the barons will have sentries on guard. None could enter, save by violence, and that we cannot allow. Should fighting occur, the attempt will be blamed on the King, and many will turn against him, saying he has broken his word of honor and become a man forsworn. The affair, if carried out, must be accomplished secretly. Why do not you, Master Clerk, steal this parchment for us? So you may earn a great reward."

"That I can not do." Timothy's voice trembled, and Gilbert knew he was afraid. "The monk or the other clerk, might wake and give the alarm, and I should be taken before I reached the barriers and surely hanged!"

"What, then, do you propose?"

"This. Before dawn, let two or three stout men-at-arms come by boat. Along the river no watch is kept. Me they must bind, so that I shall not be suspected. The monk and the other clerk can be silenced while they sleep with clubs or knives. Thus the matter can be accomplished and none the wiser. What think you, sirs?"

"How will our men know the old monk's tent?"

"I will guide them by placing a lighted taper at the door."

There was silence for a moment inside the hunting lodge. Margaret Page pressed Gilbert's hand in a small, fierce grip. Then the older of the two nobles spoke.

"Go back to Runnymead, fellow!" he said contemptuously. "Set your candle, first making sure the other two in the tent are asleep. An hour before dawn three trusted men will come. But, hark ye, we'll have no bloodshed, since thus blame and dishonor may fall upon the King. It will be your part to take the parchment from beneath the oldster's pillow and give it to our men. You need not be bound. Better if it should seem there has been no attack; that all in the tent were quietly sleeping. Thus the people's anger will not be aroused against His Majesty. Is everything understood?"

"Yes, Your Grace," Smollett muttered. "And as earnest, may I have part of the promised reward now?"

A clinking of gold pieces could be heard through the window, then the candle was extinguished and a moment later the two men, mounting their horses, rode off. Master Smollett followed, creeping like a fat ghost toward the gate.

"Now what will you do?" Margaret whispered.

"I must be at Runnymead, in bed and seeming asleep," Gilbert said, "before this traitor arrives. But how, I know not."

Margaret Page laughed, throwing back her bright blond head.

"I will take you. In our cart. Lying beneath a covering of gunny sacks you need not be seen, nor will this fat London clerk, when we pass him on the road, think aught save that countrymen bring their produce early to market. Hurry. We must harness the pony. And tell my father what is afoot. He would take you himself, were he not obliged to keep the gate."

Gilbert, nursing his painful wrist, followed the girl back to the lodge. From the stables behind it he helped her draw out a small cart and harness the pony to it. She ran into the house, returning a few moments later to say that her father was asleep and she had not awakened him.

"Leave explaining until the morrow," she said, her small chin firm. "Now we have no time. What do you propose, when you get back to the camp? Will you give the alarm?"

"No," Gilbert replied, as they drove off. "To do that would result in the men being seized, slain perhaps. The camp would be in an uproar, with everyone charging black treachery to the King. The barons will never believe that these marauders were sent without his knowledge or authority and, by reason of anger on both sides, the Charter may never be signed at all!"

"Yes." Margaret nodded. "That is true. Even now, few are willing to trust King John's word. But what other course ——"

"Leave the matter to me," Gilbert laughed, and would say no more.

Halfway to Runnymead they overtook Master Smollett, trudging steadily along the starlit road. The cart clattered by him, with Gilbert unseen beneath his cover of sacks. At the outskirts of the camp Margaret stopped. Gilbert pressed her hand, then jumped out.

"God willing," he said, "I shall see you soon again."

"Oh, do be careful," the girl murmured gravely. "I am deeply troubled, for fear some harm may come to you."

Smiling, he watched her drive off. A sleepy guard at the barrier, recognizing him, nodded. The great camp was wrapped in slumber. Gilbert made his way silently to the tent.

Inside it, he had difficulty in making out the fragile figure of Brother Anselm, asleep upon his pallet. Kneeling down, Gilbert thrust a cautious hand beneath the old monk's pillow. A faint crackle of parchment sounded, then Gilbert stood up; and having taken off shoes, breeches and doublet, stretched himself out on his own bed of straw.

After what seemed a long time, Timothy Smollett, making no sound, crept into the tent. Gilbert, watchful, snored a little, pretending to be asleep.

Timothy's first act was to crawl to Brother Anselm's side and reach beneath his pillow. Again the crackle of parchment sounded through the tent. Then Master Smollett, very slow and silent, took off his outer clothing and with flint and steel lit a small wax taper. Again assuring himself that both his companions were sleeping, he set the taper just outside the tent door. Amid the spears of grass its faint, flickering flame was no more than a tiny yellow spark. This done, Timothy, too, lay down to wait, the roll of parchment he had taken from beneath Brother Anselm's pillow now clutched in his hands.

Gilbert anxiously counted the moments. With midsummer dawn coming so early, the men must arrive very soon. At last soft footsteps on the grass told him they had come. Two shadowy figures stepped into the tent, while a third stood on guard outside. Through half-closed eyes Gilbert watched the little scene.

"Where is the parchment, fellow?" one of the men whispered grimly.

"Here." Master Smollett stood up, extended the roll in his hand. "Blow out the candle, lest you be seen. And give me my money."

The leader of the party tossed a clinking purse to the floor. He was, Gilbert thought, the knight he had seen in the wood.

"Take it, scurvy knave!" the man muttered contemptuously. "And may it bring you naught but sorrow." A moment later the candle was out, and the men had disappeared in the gloom.

Still pretending to snore, Gilbert heard Smollett crawling about through the darkness in search of his ill-gotten pay. Soon he crept back to his bed. Before the sun rose he was sleeping heavily, his loose mouth hanging wide. Careful not to awaken him, Gilbert got up, went to the old monk's side, and again thrust a hand beneath Brother Anselm's pillow. A moment later he was back on his own pallet of straw. A misty gray light showed outside the door of the tent, indicating that dawn was close at hand.

Waking early, as old men do, Brother Anselm called to his two clerks.

"Up with you, rascals!" he cried briskly. "Today we must break our fast with the sun." He reached beneath his pillow, drawing out a parchment roll. "Longer than the List of Articles," he went on, glancing at the closely scrawled page. "And four fair copies to be made. We shall need a full day at least, ere the task be completed. Make haste! Don't stand there gaping; the clerks from London will soon be here."

Timothy Smollett, halfway into his breeches, stared at the old man like a surprised and frightened fish. Through his open mouth came only a succession of meaningless grunts.

"Eh . . . eh . . . but. . . ." he floundered.

"What ails you, lad?" Brother Anselm went on. "Bestir yourself! Fetch water from the river. There is work ahead! Or are you planning, like Master Gilbert, to spend the day writing verses?"

Gilbert, although his wrist still pained him sharply, laughed.

"I shall write none," he said, "for during the night someone has stolen the parchment I meant to clean and use for that purpose." He gave Master Smollett a knowing grin. "Have you by chance seen anything of it, Timothy?"

Smollett snatched up an empty pail and staggered weakly from the tent, pursued by Gilbert's mocking laughter. Brother Anselm began to lay the table for breakfast.

Two days later, although unwillingly, King John placed his royal seal upon the Magna Carta. So in the year of our Lord 1215, was taken the first great step toward English democracy.

As the sixteenth century after Christ dawned upon earth, a great New World had just been discovered beyond the Western Ocean. From it a vast and ever increasing flood of gold poured into the coffers of ancient Spain.

Under the spur of this ravished wealth I saw a vain and cruel despot rise, dreaming of conquest in the Old World as it had been accomplished by Spaniards in the New. At his right hand stalked the mailed and bloody figure of brute force; at his left, the even more sinister and terrible shape of religious persecution. King Philip of Spain, lusting like Alexander for more worlds to conquer, now turned his eyes upon the peaceful inhabitants of the Low Countries, whose sole offense was that they were free men, worshipping God in accordance with the dictates of their conscience.

Before the century had passed I saw these innocent and peace-loving Dutch and Belgians crushed beneath a tyrant's heel, their cities ravished, their homes invaded, their women and children destroyed by fire and sword. Yet they would not bend the knee to a Spanish King, preferring death itself to slavery of body and soul.

I beheld the boldest spirits of this race, a race that even Caesar could not conquer, driven from their homeland to dwell in ships! Beggars of the sea, lacking even food to eat, so that for a time the flame of Dutch democracy burned only in the faint lamps at the mastheads of their ships, hard driven across the waters.

But while they lacked food, they were not wanting in courage. Refused safe harbor on neighboring shores at Philip's command, they returned at last to their own land and so, gaining a precarious foothold on its coast, began the long struggle to win back from the Spanish King what in the past they had won from the hungry sea. Fiercely they fought, as men ever fight who carry the flag of freedom. Watching that bitter conflict, I felt proud of my liberty-loving sons.

BEGGARS OF THE SEA

JAN TEN EYCK came into the room and sat down on a painted oak bench. Mynheer Blok was in his tulip garden, the elderly maidservant explained, but she would take him word at once.

April sunshine, drifting through the leaded panes of the window, made diamond-shaped patterns on the dark, polished floor. The quaintly carved beams of the ceiling, the massive pieces of furniture, the window frames and doors were all waxed until they shone. Blue Delft tiles lining the fireplace gave a touch of color to the otherwise sombre room.

Jan gazed about, twirling his broad-brimmed hat. He was not yet eighteen, but sturdily built, strong. The deep red-brown of his hair matched the color of the polished oak; his eyes were clear blue, like the Delft tiling.

This was the first time he had ever been inside his employer's house and even now he did not know why Mynheer Blok had sent for him, or why the little carpenter shop was closed. On ordinary days he would by this time have been busy with saw and plane helping to make chests, tables and chairs for the good burghers of Rotterdam. Something serious must have occurred. As he came along the canal he had noticed that many other shops also showed closed doors.

A clacking of wooden shoes outside the window told Jan that Mynheer Blok was at hand. He came into the room, a short, solid man wearing snuff-colored breeches and a soiled leather jerkin. For a moment he paused just inside the door-way, his broad and ruddy face drawn in a frown.

Jan stood up, awkwardly fingering his hat.

"You sent for me, Mynheer?" he asked.

Martin Blok waved him back to the bench and went to a chest along the wall. Unlocking it, he took out some coins.

"Here are the wages due you," he muttered, not unkindly.

Jan took the money, blinking.

"Does this mean, Mynheer, that I am no longer in your service?"

"Yes. For the present at least." The older man sank heavily into a chair. "Let me explain," he went on, noticing the look of dismay on Jan's face. "I need not tell you how that royal beast, King Philip of Spain, and his jackal, the Duke of Alva, hold us of the Low Countries in their cruel grip. Not only do our bodies suffer at the hands of the soldiery and the Inquisition, but our immortal souls as well! The Dutch people are being robbed, tortured, burned to death because they ask freedom and the right to worship God as they please. Young as you are, you must have seen these things!" Martin Blok's eyes suddenly blazed.

"I have seen them," Jan agreed.

"You know, too, that in addition to other heavy burdens the King has now laid a new tax upon our backs, requiring that for all goods sold of any sort one penny in each ten received must be turned over to the crown."

"Yes, Mynheer. I know that." Jan's eyes were blazing too, now.

"But it may be you do not know"—Martin Blok brought his clenched fist down upon the arm of the chair—"that rather than pay this tax, the merchants of Holland have decided to close their shops, even though they face death as a result!"

"Death?" Jan gasped, dropping his hat.

"Yes. Word came last night that by Alva's orders any who refuse to open their doors are to be hanged before them! Already, at Brussels, eighteen now face the gallows! What will happen here in Rotterdam I do not know. But since not only my life but yours as well may be in danger I think it best that you should at once return to the home of your parents at Brill!"

Jan straightened his shoulders; it was good to know that he had not been carelessly discharged.

"I am not afraid to stay here with you, Mynheer," he said quietly. "Everyone must face danger, in these terrible days. But why, since all in the Low Countries wish freedom, do we not rise up and fight this Duke of Alva and his men?"

"Alas!" Martin Blok shook his grizzled head. "We have no leader. Our beloved Prince William of Orange has been driven from the land! Along with the best blood of the country! Stripped of their possessions by these Spanish dogs, they have become wanderers. Beggars, the Duke's men contemptuously call them. Beggars of the sea."

"I've heard of them!" Jan said eagerly. "Privateers, the fisher-men tell me. Attacking the ships of Spain . . . !"

"Much more than privateers, lad! Patriots! Heroes! Who carry, aboard their small fleet of fishing craft, the hopes and aspirations of a whole people! Driven by force of arms from our shores, these brave and desperate men, unwilling to submit to rule by a Spanish king, still fly the flag of freedom upon the high seas!" Mynheer Blok, usually so calm and stolid, sprang from his chair shaking with emotion. "So long as that flag remains flying, the spirit of The Netherlands will never be crushed!"

Jan watched his employer pace nervously up and down the room.

"Tell me more, Mynheer!" he said. "I did not know. . . ."

Martin Blok turned about, his face dark with anger.

"You did not know," he went on, "that my son is aboard that fleet! Through our fisher boats I receive frequent word. He is no beggar, but a true patriot, like those with him! Their commander, Admiral van der Marck, holds a commission

from the Prince of Orange himself! Among his captains are
many noble and distinguished men . . . Brand, Van Haren,
William of Bloix, the Sieur of Treslong, whose father once
was governor of your town of Brill! One may understand *his*
hatred of the Spanish, since they murdered his own brother!
Beggars of the sea! Princes, rather! And yet hungry! Refused
food at all English ports, by order of Elizabeth, the queen!"

"I thought the English friendly to us," Jan said.

"Friendly enough . . . the people. But Philip has threatened, should aid be given to his enemies, to invade even England itself! With a great armada! Elizabeth has no choice, short
of war, and for that she is not now ready! Yet I think the
edict, to deny our people food, must have outraged the dictates of her heart."

"But . . . with naught to eat," Jan muttered, "where will
the Beggars go?"

"Who knows? To the bottom, it may be, should they meet
the war galleys of Spain. If so, they will go down fighting
bravely . . . and carrying with them the hopes of a free people, doomed to death beneath the waters of the North Sea!"
For a long moment Mynheer Blok continued his restless pacing. "I have word from my son," he went on moodily, "that
they are returning home in the hope of obtaining food somewhere along our coast!" Suddenly the old carpenter put out
his hand. "Go now, my boy!" he said. "Go back to your people at Brill. I have many things to do this sorry day! God grant
we may meet on a happier one!"

Jan, greatly moved, stepped out into the bright spring sunshine. Thoughts of Mynheer Blok hanging from a gallows before his shop filled the boy with horror, yet there seemed nothing he could do, by remaining in Rotterdam, to prevent it. He
hurried to his lodgings, threw his few possessions into a shoulder
sack. In half an hour he was on his way to Brill.

Through the cobbled square before the Groote Kerk he went,
and so to the banks of the river. Soon he was hurrying westward along the broad, tree-lined dyke that bordered the shores
of the Maas.

There were many boats in the stream—peaceful barges and
bluff fishing craft. The broad meadows on either side were like
green velvet under the bright morning sun. Everywhere he
could see pleasant homes, grazing cattle, dogs drawing their
small, two-wheeled carts, larger wagons, and off in the pearl-
gray distance countless moving windmills, their gaunt arms
black against the misty sky. A well-ordered country, yet over
it all like a shadow hung the dark clouds of oppression, of
religious intolerance, of a tyranny that crushed the souls of
men.

Jan had a walk of some twenty miles ahead of him before
reaching Maaslandsluis near the mouth of the river, from which
point a ferry crossed to Brill. He ate bread, cheese and milk at
a tavern along the way; the landlord heard his story of the
intended hanging of shopkeepers without surprise.

"The Spaniards do not spare us," he said simply. "But with
God's help we shall endure."

Early in the afternoon Jan came to Maaslandsluis. The ferry-man, Peter Kopplestok, was dozing in his broad, flat-bottomed skiff. A native of Brill, Jan knew him well.

"Ho, Master Ten Eyck!" he said, reaching for his oars, "so you come home at Eastertide, eh? To spend the holidays with your people! They will be glad."

"I did not come for a holiday," he said.

The ferryboat slipped swiftly through the water. Jan, in its bow, stared ahead. Suddenly his keen eyes made out a group of vessels approaching the mouth of the river from the sea—at least a score, none of great size.

"Look, Peter!" he called over his shoulder. "A fleet of ships coming in! What do you make of them?"

Kopplestok turned, shading his eyes.

"Dutch!" he muttered. "Not merchant craft, since such do not sail in flotillas!" For a moment he sat resting on his oars. "If those are guns I see aboard the leading vessel, we are about to receive a visit from the Beggars of the Sea!"

Jan nodded, remembering the message Mynheer Blok had received from his son. The leading ship, a sturdy craft of some two hundred tons burden, was headed directly toward them, with a man in her bows making signals, waving his arms.

"I think you're right, Peter," Jan said. "What do you sup-pose they want with us?"

"We'd best find out." The ferryman bent over his long ash sweeps, drove the boat rapidly ahead. "As good Dutchmen we must render them any service we can."

As they neared the leading vessel, Jan saw a tall, handsome man in gray doublet and breeches lean over the rail.

"It's the Lord of Treslong, William of Bloix," Kopplestok grunted. "You should know him, lad, since he lived at Brill while his father was governor."

The man at the rail waved his plumed hat.

"Ho . . . Kopplestok!" he called out. "Come alongside. I must speak to you."

The ferryman shot his craft into the vessel's lee.

"Take the boathook and hold us fast," he said to Jan.

Treslong's tanned face was lean from hunger, but it still wore a gay and defiant smile.

"Are you a good and loyal patriot, Master Kopplestok?" he cried.

"None better, Captain, as I think you know!" The ferry-man's broad features broke into a grin. "What can I do for you?"

"Help us to get food; we are starving."

Jan, gripping the boathook to keep the skiff from drifting, looked up. A row of grim, haggard faces lined the rail, clean-shaven, for the most part, except for their long, fierce mus-taches. The men were all dressed in gray, the color used by beggars throughout the Low Countries. They had adopted this costume, noble and commoner alike, since the scornful words of the Duke of Alva's lieutenant, Berlaymont. Better to be beggars, than kneel to the Spanish King.

"Starving, Captain?" Kopplestok called back. "That is bad.

There is food aplenty in Brill but I doubt if any will sell to you, for fear of the Duke and his men."

Captain Treslong laughed, a bitter, sardonic laugh.

"I do not expect them to. Nor indeed have we money where' with to buy. So it seems we must take what we need."

"But, Mynheer. . . . Brill is a strong and well-fortified place."

"And we are strong and very hungry men!" Treslong waved to the twenty-odd vessels behind him. "Our commander in chief, Admiral van der Marck, wishes to send a message to the Governor and magistrates of Brill! I told him I knew a brave and loyal man who would take it! So I came on ahead . . . in search of you."

"But . . . but," Kopplestok objected, "they would pay no attention to any message that I, a poor ferryman, might bring."

Treslong drew a signet ring from his finger, tossing it into the boat.

"Show them this!" he cried. "They know well the crest carved on it, from the days when my father governed the town! Tell them that our Admiral, Count van der Marck, in the name of Prince William of Orange, demands the immediate surrender of Brill!"

"God help us!" the ferryman muttered. "I shall be boiled in oil for this!"

"Tell them also," Treslong went on, "to send deputies at once to talk over the terms. If our demands are not accepted within two hours, we shall attack!"

Kopplestok picked up the ring and put it on his little finger —the only one it would fit.

"Cast off, lad!" he called to Jan. "We have work ahead!"

Peter released the boathook, deeply troubled. Brill to be at' tacked . . . with his father and mother inside its walls! He glanced back. The Lord of Treslong, a smiling and gallant fig' ure, stood waving his plumed beaver hat. With the wind blow' ing his long, fair locks, his head held high, he seemed to Jan the very spirit of a brave and dauntless people.

Kopplestok, his brawny shoulders bent over the oars, sent his skiff flying toward the harbor. Along the wharves that lined the dyke were groups of men, burghers and magistrates who had come out to see what the arrival of this fleet of ships meant. At the north gate of the town, and on the walls above it, a few Spanish pikemen leaned idly upon their weapons, watching the scene.

The ferryboat slid alongside one of the piers, and Jan held it fast with his boathook while Kopplestok spoke to the group above.

"I come with a message from the Lord of Treslong, whose ship you see there in the river!" he announced, holding up a broad red hand. "As a token, here is his signet!" He flashed the heavy seal ring.

"What message?" a bearded magistrate asked.

"That in the name of our liege lord, Prince William of Orange, and of Admiral van der Marck, commander of the Dutch fleet, you surrender the city to him at once!"

"The Beggars of the Sea!" the magistrate gasped, suddenly grown pale. In whispers he and his companions consulted.

Jan, looking on, well understood their dilemma. Most were good patriots, favoring the Prince of Orange and his cause, but they also feared the vengeance that Alva and his men might take upon them for giving aid to any opposing the power of Spain. Should Brill open its gates to these rebels, troops sent quickly from the garrisons at Rotterdam or Utrecht would put these honest burghers and their families to the sword, the rack, the stake. Small wonder the magistrates hesitated. As news of what was happening spread back through the town, hundreds began to flee from it by way of the south gate, carrying their most prized possessions with them.

The discussion among the magistrates dragged on interminably. Messengers were sent back and forth between them and the Governor. Jan, eager to get away and see his parents, was warned that until the matter had been settled, he could not leave the boat. Meanwhile, the other ships of the Beggars' fleet sailed into the harbor—twenty-four all told.

At last a panting burgher arrived with the Governor's final word. Two deputies were to go aboard the Admiral's ship, agree to furnish him with ample supplies of food, provided he would promise to sail away as soon as it had been received. The magistrates selected were about to step into Kopplestok's skiff.

By this time, however, the two hours had been exhausted, and also the Admiral's patience. He ordered his fighting men into their boats. The burghers and magistrates, seeing a swarm of small craft approaching the docks, hastily retreated inside the walls of the town.

Jan's sympathies were all with the Beggars. He hoped that the help he and Kopplestok had given them might serve as a means to keep harm from his parents during any attack upon the town. But when he saw the small number of fighting men, less than two hundred, that landed from the boats he doubted that such an attack could be successful. He noticed, however, that some of the ships, led by Captain Treslong, had sailed farther up the river, planning, no doubt, to assault the south gate at the same time.

A group of the Beggars came along the dock led by a tall, powerful man with a fierce, heavily-bearded face and dark, unkempt hair. He looked to Jan like a pirate.

"That is Van der Marck!" Peter Kopplestok muttered. "A relative of his, Count Egmont, was murdered by Alva's orders, and the Admiral, I am told, has sworn not to trim his hair or beard until Egmont's death has been avenged."

The commander of the Beggars stopped, gazed down into the boat.

"Are you Kopplestok—the one who brought my message?" he asked.

"Yes." The ferryman held up Treslong's crested ring.

"What was the Governor's reply?"

"That your ships be provided with food, on condition you sail away. . . ."

"Too late!" Van der Marck turned to his men. "Gather fire-wood!" he ordered. "Pile it against the gate! We will burn our way in! Find also a stout timber, to be used as a battering-ram!"

The Beggars scattered, ripping planks from the wharves, tearing spars, decking from nearby fisher boats, smashing other small craft. Soon a great mass of wood had been piled against the massive iron-barred gate. A score of men arrived carrying between them a ship's mast, as thick through as a good-sized tree. The fire was lighted and smoke and flames, billowing up, drove the few armed guards from the wall above. Presently the Beggars, advancing with their ram, began to batter the twisting metal of the gate with heavy blows.

Jan leaped from the boat, fear for his parents gnawing at his heart.

"I'm going into the town!" he cried.

"How?" Kopplestok followed him; he had a wife inside the walls.

"I know a way! Come along!"

The ferryman looped the painter of his boat around the top of a pile, then ran after Jan down the river dyke. A broad causeway at the top of it skirted the east walls of the town. To Jan all the paths and byways about Brill had been an open book since early boyhood. Having reached a point opposite one of the towers that stood at intervals along the gray stone ram-parts, he leaped from the causeway—Kopplestok panting at his heels—and came to a rusty iron grating set low in the walls.

A score of men arrived carrying a ship's mast.

He had often used it in the past as a short cut to and from the river, and he prayed now that the broken bolt had not been repaired.

Eagerly he grasped the moss-grown bars, swinging the grating outward. Beyond lay a small tunnel, piercing the thickness of the wall, and built to carry off rain water in time of storms.

"I'll never get through," Kopplestok groaned. "My shoulders are too broad."

"Try it!" Jan called back, as he began to crawl through the opening.

The tunnel was slippery with mud and slime, but in a few moments he emerged inside the walls of the town. Kopplestok followed, puffing and swearing, his crimson face streaked with grime. Jan took the ferryman's hands, helping him up.

"My father's house is in the next street," he said. "That is how I knew about the tunnel. We'll stop there first, then go on to the south gate—help Captain Treslong and his men!"

The town seemed absolutely deserted now that most of the people had fled, but in front of the pleasant brick house toward which Jan led the way several men were standing.

Being engaged in a lively discussion, they did not at once notice him and Kopplestok.

One of the group, a thin, gray-haired burgher, was speaking in a high, harsh voice.

"You are a fool, Mynheer Ten Eyck!" he exclaimed. "Staying here with pirates and freebooters at our gates! Come, you and your good wife, while there is yet time. . . ."

Then Jan saw his father standing just inside the doorway, with his mother a little beyond. Cornelius Ten Eyck, stalwart and cool-eyed, shook his head.

"Not pirates, Friend Dietz," he corrected, "but good patriots who deserve our help. Why should I fear them?"

"You should fear the Spaniards!" the gray-haired man retorted. "I am told that the Governor himself is about to leave in his carriage to summon quick aid. When the troops get here, any who have assisted these freebooters will be flayed alive!"

"Still I shall remain," Mynheer Ten Eyck replied steadily. Raising his eyes, he caught sight of the two mud-begrimed figures in the street. "Jan!" he cried out. "What are you doing here?"

Jan ran to the door, kissed his mother, pressed his father's hand.

"No time to explain now!" he said. "Peter Kopplestok and I are on our way to the south gate, to let Captain Treslong and his men in!" He watched Dietz and his companions hurry off. "We may be in time to stop the Governor as well!"

"I'll go with you, Son!" Mynheer Ten Eyck said quickly. "Once he is outside the walls, with fast horses, and there will be no way to prevent him from reaching Rotterdam!"

The three ran swiftly. As they turned into the street leading to the south gateway, they saw a coach with liveried servants on the box lumbering over the cobblestones ahead of them.

"The Governor's carriage!" Mynheer Ten Eyck cried. "Come on!"

At top speed they passed it. Jan caught sight of a pale-faced man inside, surrounded by boxes and bundles. He had a great silver chain about his neck.

Two pikemen stood on guard at the gateway. Seeing the Governor approaching, one of them sprang to raise the beam that barred the heavy gate. The other, supposing Jan and his companions to be citizens eager to escape, thrust out his pike.

"Stand aside," he ordered roughly, "until His Excellency's coach has passed!"

Instead of obeying, Jan seized the pike shaft. The man, expecting nothing of the sort, allowed the weapon to be wrenched from his grasp. The guard trying to open the gate had set his pike against the wall in order to leave his hands free. Mynheer Ten Eyck sprang forward and seized it.

"Into the guardhouse with them!" he shouted, nodding toward a narrow doorway in one of the gate towers. A moment later the two unarmed men had been driven through it and the door closed, with Kopplestok, knife in hand, on guard outside.

Then Jan and his father were facing the Governor and his servants behind the blades of their long, deadly pikes.

His Excellency, white with anger, leaned from the coach. Its horses, suddenly checked, danced madly upon the cobbles.

"Open the gate!" he cried. "I must get away . . . for help!"

Jan and his father did not move.

"Why should you stop me?" the Governor went on. "Do you not know that murderers and cutthroats are threatening the town? Already they are at the north gate! At any moment they may attack from the south, and escape be cut off!"

His Excellency had barely completed the sentence when shouts sounded outside the walls, followed at once by a thunder of blows against the massive, iron-bound gate. Deserting his post before the guardhouse door, Peter Kopplestok ran to lift the great oak bar. Setting one of his powerful shoulders beneath it, he gave a mighty heave. An instant later the Beggars, led by Captain Treslong, surged into the town.

Seeing Jan and Peter Kopplestok, Treslong laughed.

"Well done, lads!" he shouted, "although how you got in ahead of me is a mystery I must hear about later!" His merry eyes caught sight of the Governor, sitting furious in the coach. "Ah . . . Your Excellency! Greetings! It would appear that we arrived just in time. Do not touch him, or his goods," he went on to his followers. "Remember, we are not here to pillage! Van Hoorn . . . see that the Governor is taken back to his house in safety—and kept there! Wirtz . . . lead your men to the north gate, in case the Admiral should need help! Let a dozen remain on guard here, but leave the gateway open so that the good people of Brill, seeing we mean them no harm, may return in peace to their homes."

Jan introduced his father, and Kopplestok returned the Lord of Treslong his signet ring, telling him how they had crawled through the drain.

"For our services, Captain," the ferryman said, "I hope no harm will come to our families. I have a wife. . . ."

"Have no fear, my friends!" he replied. "We may be hungry, but we are not wolves, only good patriots, fighting for our Prince's cause. No harm will come to any who support the House of Orange! Come, let us see how matters have gone at the north gate."

Long before they had reached it, however, the question was answered. Near the center of the town they came upon Admiral van der Marck, standing with some of his men. The Admiral's fierce, bearded face was smoke-blackened, his gray cloak covered with soot and ashes, but there was a smile in his eyes.

"Ho, William!" he said to Treslong. "We have the place, it seems!"

"With God's help, yes!" Treslong replied. "And the Governor as well, thanks to this lad and his friends. I think we had best interview His Excellency at once." Waving his hat, the Lord of Treslong strode off at Van der Marck's side, and Jan and his father, leaving Kopplestok, went back to the house. Everywhere along the way they met groups of the Beggars carrying loaves of bread, cheese, and other food in their hands. Orders had been given to spare the homes of the people of Brill, but nothing could prevent these starving men from looting the shops.

Over supper that night Jan told his father and mother all that had occurred since his departure from Rotterdam in the morning. Mynheer Ten Eyck shook his head.

"Even though the Governor was stopped," he said, "news of this matter will quickly spread, and we shall have troops here ready to retake the town and put us all to the sword. But we could do naught else than what we have done, and must endure to the end, placing our faith in God!"

"He is our strength and our fortress," Jan's mother, a silvery-haired, patient woman, said quietly. "And He will not desert us in the hour of need."

The soldiers of the Duke did indeed arrive, in spite of the Governor's failure to escape. Three days later a fleet of small galleys and barges appeared in the river with ten companies of pikemen from the garrison at Utrecht, led by Count Bossu, one of the Duke's most able commanders. The fate of Brill seemed sealed.

The Beggars, however, had not been idle. Aided by patriotic townsmen, most of whom had returned to their homes, the gates of the city were repaired, cannon from the fleet were mounted on the ramparts, and everything was made ready for a siege.

Jan, who had been helping to build gun carriages for the cannon, watched the Spaniards disembark. From where he stood on the ramparts it was possible to obtain a view of the whole scene. Company by company these veteran pikemen, said to be the best soldiers in Europe, marched from the quays into the low meadows surrounding the north side of the town.

Peter Kopplestok, leaning over the parapet, grunted.

"They're sending a messenger with a flag of truce," he said, "demanding, no doubt, surrender at once. I know what the Admiral will tell them."

A little later news spread along the walls that Van der Marck had laughed in the messenger's face, and that the Spanish were preparing to attack the north gate.

Jan picked up his carpenter's axe, slipped it under his belt.

"If the Nieuland sluice were opened, Peter, those Spaniards in the meadow would either have to retreat or be drowned."

"True enough," Kopplestok agreed. "But how get to it?"

Jan pointed to a coil of rope used for raising the heavy cannon to the walls.

"If you will let me down on the river side," he said, "I could swim to the sluice . . . I think." An instant later he had seized the rope and was running along the wall.

The Spaniards, busy about the north gate, did not see Jan's small figure as he was lowered from the ramparts to the river dyke. Plunging in, he swam with the tide until he reached the wooden sluice, cut it through with half a dozen swift blows of his axe. A moment later, still unseen, he was swimming back again, to be pulled by Kopplestok to the top of the wall.

By this time a broad stream of water was pouring into the meadows at the north of the town. The Spaniards, becoming aware of it, made frantic efforts to repair the break but the current was far too strong. Soon, realizing that they were in danger of being overwhelmed by the rapidly rising flood, they abandoned their attack on the north gate and scrambled back to the top of the dyke.

Shots from the direction of the south gate sent Jan and Peter racing along the ramparts toward it. They found that another group of pikemen making an assault there had just been driven back in disorder by a devastating blast of cannon fire from the Beggars' guns on the wall. But the Spaniards who had left the fields at the north of the town were now streaming down the causeway on top of the dyke to reinforce their comrades to the south.

Captain Treslong was watching them from the ramparts when Jan and Peter Kopplestok raced up.

"Why have they left the north gate?" he asked.

"Driven out by water," Jan said. "The Nieuland sluice has been cut."

Without stopping to ask who had cut it, Treslong brought his fist down on the parapet.

"Kopplestok!" he shouted. "Where is your boat?"

"Tied alongside a wharf at the river front."

"Can you get to it . . . now that the north gate is free?"

"No doubt. But I may have to swim, since the meadows are flooded. But why . . . ?"

Treslong turned to the men about him.

"Louden," he said, "keep the Spaniards off with your guns! In another hour it will be dark! Hook . . . Roobol . . . come with me! Bring slow matches . . . oil-soaked rags . . . pitch!"

"But, Captain," one of the Beggars asked, "what are you planning to do?"

"Go out on the river! In Kopplestok's boat. We can reach it, now that the north gate is clear. Under cover of darkness we shall row to the Spanish fleet of barges, set them afire, or cut them adrift! God has delivered the enemy into our hands! Come, Kopplestok!"

"May I go, too?" Jan asked.

"He deserves it, Captain," the ferryman grunted, "for having cut the Nieuland sluice. . . ."

Treslong took Jan by the arm.

"Of course, lad," he said. "In fact I hereby make you a member of our company—a true Beggar of the Sea!"

The little group, hurrying to the north gate, found no difficulty in leaving it. Except for a rising flood of water, the way to the docks was clear. In the distance a few Spaniards could be seen, racing southward along the dyke.

Wading through water up to their armpits, Treslong and his band reached the pier at which Kopplestok's boat was tied. They tumbled aboard, lay flat on the floor, while the ferryman drove the light craft through the gathering darkness toward the cluster of masthead lamps that marked the position of the Spanish fleet. It lay close to shore, but the guards posted on the causeway, not expecting attack from the water side, were watching the movements of their forces about the south gate.

As Kopplestok sculled his boat along the edge of the silent flotilla, barge after barge was set afire or cut loose by the slashing knives of Captain Treslong and his crew. The few sailors left aboard the fleet were too surprised by the sudden and unexpected attack to offer much resistance. Before the guards on the causeway realized what was happening, over half the Spanish vessels were either aflame where they lay or were drifting helplessly downstream with the tide.

At sight of their blazing fleet, Count Bossu's men fell into a desperate panic. Between the flood of water rolling down upon them from the northern meadows, and the fire that threat- ened to cut off their escape by sea, they abandoned all thought of taking the town and began a wild scramble along the dyke. Hundreds, pushed from the narrow and overcrowded cause- way, fell into the river and were drowned, while those who remained were subjected to a murderous fire from the guns upon the walls. Only a small part of Bossu's ten companies managed to reach the remaining boats and make good their escape.

That night the citizens of Brill, called together by Admiral van der Marck, swore allegiance to the Prince of Orange. The Beggars had gained a foothold on the soil of their native land.

"Now at last," the Lord of Treslong said to Jan, "the Dutch Republic is new born. From here, God willing, we shall fight on until all Holland is once more under our flag!"

All through the war-torn years of the seventeenth and eighteenth centuries I watched the beacon fires of liberty burn ever more brightly over Europe, from the peaks of the Alps in Switzerland to the dykes of the Low Countries; from the pleasant hillsides of England to the southernmost shores of France.

I saw the new Dutch Republic rise to splendid achievement under the rule of free and courageous men. I saw the Great Armada of Philip the Conqueror, defeated by the wooden walls of England, creep back to Spain, broken. I watched sturdy Swiss mountaineers throw off a foreign yoke as their great patriot, Arnold von Winkleried, gathering the lances of the Austrian knights to his breast, opened the way to victory at the Battle of Sempach. I saw the people of England rise against King Charles, as they had centuries before risen against King John, to assert the right of Parliament to make the nation's laws. And in France, where peasants lived like cattle under a stupid King and a vicious and pleasure-loving Court, I heard men everywhere asking why the many should starve to gratify the vanities of an idle few.

But it was across a great ocean that I saw the lamps of liberty burn with their clearest and most brilliant flame. There freedom-loving men from many lands had gathered, seeking the right to live, to speak, to worship God as they pleased. Hunger and cold and the arrows of savage enemies they had faced, and were now declaring a doctrine of equality, of democracy, in words that can never fade so long as love of freedom burns in the hearts of men.

Proudly I watched them year after year, as they fought and died for the right to life, liberty and the pursuit of happiness. Fought not only against foes who assailed them from without, but against even more cunning and insidious enemies from within. Enemies who struck at their leader Washington himself, and but for an unknown woman might have brought disaster to the patriot cause. Perhaps the God to whom that great leader prayed in the snows of Valley Forge held out a protecting hand, not wishing the battle for democracy to be lost.

ENEMIES FROM WITHIN

THE slim young girl in faded gingham made a charming picture as she went through the tavern garden swinging her
wooden pail.

There were apple trees around the well and a small, sweet
breeze from the south blew pink petals over the flagstones, scattering some of them into the girl's bright, corn-colored hair.
She sang as she turned the windlass and brought up the brim-
ming oak bucket. It was easy to sing on an evening in June,
when one was just eighteen. Beyond the trees she could see the
roofs and chimney pots of buildings stretching down along the
Broad Way as far as the Battery.

Suddenly the girl turned. A tall young man was coming
through the trees toward her, breathing heavily, as though he

had been running. He wore the buff and blue of a Continental soldier, and his rugged, sunburnt face was flushed and eager.

"I hurried," he said, "to get ahead of that rascal Tom Hickey. He's off duty tonight, too. From what I hear, you've been walking out with him. . . ."

"Is it so?" the girl's blue eyes flashed dangerously. "And what call have you, Master Bradford, to spy upon my comings and goings? Or tell me with whom I may spend my spare time? Tom Hickey's a fine figure of a man."

"So many women have found him. I hope his good looks and his blarney haven't turned your silly head."

"So you think me silly?" Her chin snapped up.

"Yes . . . if you listen to his cunning lies. The fellow is a scoundrel, and means you no good. . . ."

"And what good do *you* mean, Jim Bradford? I have yet to hear. . . ."

"Oh, Ellen, you know very well I love you . . . and hope to marry you when, when. . . ." He hesitated, stumbling.

"Indeed." The girl's lips curled disdainfully. "And so to prove your love you call me silly and object because I speak to another man."

"How can I do more, with only a soldier's pay . . . and that in worthless script. When the war is ended, I hope. . . ."

"La . . . la, Master Bradford. Would you measure love in terms of shillings and pence? Tom Hickey is more gallant."

"No doubt he offers kisses instead." Jim Bradford's face hardened. "Take care, Ellen, that they do not prove base coin."

Before the girl could reply, another uniformed figure joined them at the well. A slender, jaunty man of thirty, whose bold blue eyes and flashing smile contrasted sharply with Jim Bradford's angry frowns. Although their uniforms were the same, Tom Hickey managed to invest his with the authority of a general.

"My respects to you, Mistress Ellen," he said, with a gay laugh. Then his eyes turned to Jim Bradford. "What now, Master Spoilsport? Must you ruin this sweet maid's evening with your scowls? Cheer up, lad! Find yourself another sweetheart. Mistress Ellen is not one to waste her time with kill-joys."

From a rear window of the tavern came a shrill voice.

"Hurry with the water, you lazy wench!" it cried. "Must I be kept waiting all the evening?"

Tom Hickey picked up the girl's pail.

"Come, darlin'," he said. "Faith, 'tis a pleasure to serve you . . . and take you away from this sour-faced lad. Shall we walk out tonight, when your tasks are done? There will be a fine moon. . . ."

The two made a charming picture, as they went up the flagstone path.

Jim Bradford, however, staring moodily after them, did not find it so. How could a man ask a girl to marry him when he had no money? Tom Hickey had none, either, but marriage, Jim felt sure, did not enter into his calculations. A pretty girl, to amuse him—to be kissed, under the moon. Jim sank to a bench beside one of the apple trees, sat with his head in his

"—and what call have you to spy on my comings and goings?"

hands, staring at the ground. Why, he groaned in helpless anger, did he always say the wrong things, leaving a worthless ne'er-do-well like Hickey to say the right ones? In his preoccupation he did not see the stalwart man in a white laced coat who appeared through the shrubbery.

Master Forbes, the gunsmith, making his way toward the side door of the tavern, paused for a few moments behind a clump of lilac bushes to watch the little scene about the well. To his crafty eyes a lover's quarrel presented distinct possibilities—especially one involving a brace of young soldiers.

All that afternoon Master Forbes had tramped the streets of New York upon an important mission. It had nothing to do, however, with the sale of guns or other such lethal weapons, being concerned rather with a matter of bounties, and dark oaths to be sworn, together with the finding of men to swear them, reckless and desperate men, of a kind to be come by in beer halls and taverns and other such resorts of the unregenerate.

Wherefore Master Forbes, after successfully offering his wares at the sign of the Highlander, on Beaver Street, at the beerhouse of fat Sam Lowry, near the Oswego Market, and at Jim Houlding's popular bar, so providentially close to the powder magazines of the Upper Barracks, had now returned to his lair at Tom Corbie's new tavern, a scant eighth of a mile from the Richmond Hill mansion at which General Washington had established his headquarters.

The day had been sultry, and Master Forbes, because of the frequent noggins of rum forced on him by the nature of his business that afternoon, was overheated. He strode to the well, filled a long-handled dipper from the dripping bucket.

"A warm day, young man," he said to Jim. "Won't you join me in a cup of fresh water? Or, if you prefer a mug of ale in the taproom. . . ." He nodded toward the tavern.

"I'm not thirsty," Jim Bradford replied.

Nothing daunted, Master Forbes came to the bench and sat down.

"A soldier, I see," he commented. "From General Washington's headquarters, no doubt." His eyes swept the broad meadows beyond which lay the mansion at Richmond Hill. "Do they still pay you in shinplasters and promises?"

"Money is scarce," Jim admitted.

"Too scarce, no doubt," Master Forbes added craftily, "for a man to marry. I am told, however"—he assumed a paternal air—"of ways by which an enterprising young fellow can come by not only a good round sum in gold, but two hundred acres of fine farming land—even three hundred, if he be married. Enough to make himself a home, become his own master. . . ."

"How may that be?" Jim Bradford asked, suddenly alert. "Do you make such an offer?"

"Not I. My trade is that of a gunsmith. But in going about the town I hear much gossip. The offer, 'tis said, is made by Governor Tryon, now in refuge on a ship in the harbor. He seeks to enlist recruits who will remain faithful to the King of England."

"Tories, in other words," Jim grunted.

"Why not? Although 'Loyalists' is the word they prefer. There are many not only in New York but throughout the country who do not hold with General Washington's views, and call those who follow him rebels. Should his uprising against King George fail, matters are likely to go hard with them. Many will doubtless be hanged as traitors. I am a man of peace, and take no part in such controversies, but I am in' formed that many hereabouts are accepting the Governor's bounty."

Jim Bradford's scowl darkened.

"And for these gifts of money and land," he inquired, "what sevice is to be rendered in return?"

"I understand"—Master Forbes' eyes strongly suggested those of a dead fish—"that such information is not given until the new recruit, having accepted the bounty in gold, first swears a solemn oath of secrecy, forfeiting his life should he break it." He watched the young soldier narrowly. "May I ask, sir, your name?"

"Bradford. James Bradford. I am a member of General Wash' ington's bodyguard."

The gunsmith made a sudden decision.

"If you are really interested, young man," he said, "I may be able to give you further information before the evening is over. Come and see me, here at the tavern, later on. Inquire for me through the proprietor, Tom Corbie. My name is Gil' bert Forbes." The gunsmith rose, smiling, and strode up the path. As he reached the side door of the tavern, he saw Jim

Bradford rise from the bench and start despondently across Mr. Lispenard's meadows toward the Broad Way.

Inside the tavern Forbes came upon Tom Corbie's mulatto servant, Jasper.

"Tell your master I have gone to my private quarters, boy," he said. "Ask him to attend me there as soon as may be." Master Forbes quickly mounted the stairs.

Tom Corbie came into the room, carefully closing the door behind him.

"What now?" he asked, wiping beery fingers on his leather apron. "I have no further word from the Governor to add to the letter Jasper brought ashore from the ship yesterday." The tavern keeper seemed disturbed; beads of sweat covered his broad pumpkin-red face. "I deem it unwise for us to meet so often."

"Nonsense, man." Master Forbes set his broad back against the mantelpiece. "Who is there to hear, or see? The letter Jasper brought contained final instructions. They are to have everything in readiness, against the arrival from Boston of Lord Howe's fleet. A matter of days, our worthy Mayor says. I suppose you know he has been persuaded to join the plot. Here are the names of four men who may come, seeking me." He handed Corbie a bit of paper. "They are reckless scoundrels, who will be used to shoot the officers and set fire to the powder magazine at the Upper Barracks. And now we come to the most important matter of all—the securing, without delay, of dependable agents among Washington's personal bodyguard."

Corbie shook his head. "They be all picked men, I hear, and faithful."

"None of these rascally rebels is faithful, if caught in liquor and offered a good round sum. Once they have accepted the Governor's bounty, been sworn upon the Book, we have them, body and soul."

"Well?" the innkeeper asked grimly. "What's your plan?"

"There is one of the General's bodyguard, I am informed, who visits your taproom regularly. A handsome young Irish-man named Hickey. Do you know the fellow?"

"Aye. Tom Hickey. A strong and fearless lad, but overfond of the women . . . and his whiskey."

"Good! We must get him for the King."

"And how will you go about it?"

"First, through the bottle. Second, and more important, by the fact that he is a deserter from the British Army."

"That should make him stick all the closer to the rebels."

"Being a traitor to the British already," Master Forbes observed sourly, "he has no cause, save his own. A man who turns his coat once will do so again, if it be to his advantage. The Governor offers, to all who accept his bounty, a full pardon from the King. Your Master Hickey can add that to the two hundred acres of land for himself, a hundred for his wife, and fifty for each of his children."

"Tom Hickey has no wife, nor children. . . ."

"But he has a sweetheart, friend Corbie," Forbes went on. "One of the serving wenches here in your tavern."

"Aye. A decent enough lass. Hickey of late has been sparking her, but I doubt he has any thought of marriage."

"The Governor's offer may change his mind. Master Hickey might do worse than take a wife along with his pardon, and so gain the extra acres of land. A fool if he didn't, say I—the British give short shrift to deserters. Is the fellow now in your tap-room? I am informed he should be off duty this evening."

"He's here, drinking with some of his companions."

"Good. Now this is what you are to do. First, send the wench to fetch him, pretending some business of her own. It is important that those with him should have no knowledge of this affair. Once out, bring the fellow here to me, saying merely that a gentleman wished to see him privately. Then send up lemons, sugar, and a bottle of your best rum. It might be wise to have the wench serve us, instead of another; if Hickey is her sweetheart, she will keep a close mouth. Attend to this at once."

Corbie stepped out to the hall, bawled orders over the banisters. In a moment he was back again.

"I don't like the business," he croaked.

"We must step carefully," the gunsmith agreed.

"If we don't, we're likely to find ourselves treading on air . . . at a rope's end."

Master Forbes gave him a look of contempt.

"When Howe arrives with the fleet and ten thousand troops of the line, it will be these insolent rebels, not us, who will find themselves stretching ropes."

The tavern keeper glanced at the list of names in his hand.

"You wish to see these men when they come?"

"Yes. Privately, of course, and alone. And there may be an-other. A young fellow named Bradford. He also is a member of Washington's bodyguard. Do you know the man?"

"Slightly. A serious lad. You'll never get him by drink. He used to come here often, but not to sit in the taproom."

"Why, then?"

"To walk out with this girl Tom Hickey is sparking."

"I see . . . I see." Master Forbes smiled, nodded. The little scene he had witnessed about the tavern well now became crystal clear. "I've had a talk with Bradford. He's coming to see me later. I have ways to land him you don't know of. Leave the matter to me. What's keeping that wench you sent for?"

Corbie turned, went toward the door. The girl who stood with wide, horrified eyes in the hall outside, hearing the knob turn, rapped resolutely on one of the thin pine panels.

The General sat before his desk in the large well-furnished library which he used as a study at Richmond Hill. He laid down his pen and shook a little sand over the page of the letter he had just completed. While the ink was drying he turned to gaze into the garden.

A quarter moon, poised above the top of a tall cedar, made him think of a slice of sweet cantaloupe . . . such as grew in his Virginia fields. A perfume of honeysuckle, drifting in through the open window, carried him in an instant three hun-

dred miles to the southward; there would be honeysuckle at
Mount Vernon, too, at this season of the year.

The room was singularly quiet; Richmond Hill, in its pleasant grove of trees, seemed remote from the city so short a distance away. The surrounding oaks had once been part of
Bayard's Woods, before the town, marching steadily northward between its confining rivers, had crossed Mr. Lispenard's
broad meadows as far as Master Corbie's new tavern, the
lights of which were visible through the trees.

With a sigh the General turned back to his unfinished letter.
No time now to dream of June nights on the Potomac; more
serious matters were demanding his attention along the Hud-
son. Not only the threat of Howe's great fleet, so soon to
appear, but subtler dangers: dark Tory plots, aimed, so rumor
said, at his life and the complete destruction of the revolutionary cause. Frowning, he read the words he had written.

"It is, I think, a self-evident fact, and one indeed supported
by history, that democracies have more to fear from enemies
within, than from those who attack from without. Our struggle
to establish here in the New World a government in which
liberty, justice, and the rights of free men will ever be para-
mount cannot fail if our people are as one in their determination to resist. In spite of the strength of the enemy—and it is
great—we shall with God's help gain the victory if all will
faithfully support our just cause. But we are divided and
weakened by dissention, and by the efforts of those amongst us
who, under the cloak of moderation and compromise, are in

truth but traitors, seeking our defeat. There can be no compromise with the forces of injustice and tyranny. We must
fight on, united, until our goal of freedom has been attained.
Tell those young men who have come to you seeking advice
that they should be eternally vigilant against all plots and
strategems by which our strength may be undermined. Here
in New York are many who still urge allegiance to the King,
and I am being constantly advised of projected attempts,
against not only our cause, but against my own person. These
efforts I trust will with determination be overcome, and those
guilty of them rendered helpless. I am grateful for your words
of encouragement, and your renewal of our declaration made
at Philadelphia, that in this great struggle we have pledged to
one another our fortunes, our sacred honor and our lives. . . ."

A knock at the door caused him to turn. The officer in command of the watch appeared to report. A woman, he said—a
young girl—had been apprehended while entering the garden.
She seemed in a state of excitement and insisted on being taken
to the General at once. Her name she refused to give, nor would
she state the nature of her business except to say that it was
most important to the patriot cause. Searched, she was found
to be unarmed. If the General wished to give any special instructions. . . .

Washington considered the matter, his fine face grave.

"Very well," he said at length. "I will hear what the young
lady has to say."

The officer's eyebrows went up.

"Scarcely a lady, sir," he began.

"Never mind, if she be a good patriot, Lieutenant; I have known many ladies who were not." Washington was smiling now. "Show her in."

The slender young girl who appeared in the doorway seemed frightened. Her features were scarcely visible, since in spite of the warmth of the evening her head and shoulders were muffled in a shabby black shawl. The General, regarding her fragile and trembling figure, thought of a timid child.

"Wait outside," he told the two men at the door. "Sit down, my dear," he went on, giving his visitor an encouraging smile.

The girl sank into a chair, her fingers twisting the ragged fringe of her shawl. Her breath came in short gasps, as if she had been running, but her cheeks, instead of showing color, were ash pale.

"Who are you?" the General went on in a gentle voice, "and why do you wish to see me?"

"Oh sir . . . your Excellency . . . never mind my name. I am afeard anyone should know it, or learn I've been here. I work at Corbie's tavern, and have only a little time before I may be missed. I came to tell you about the plot. . . ."

"What plot?" The General's eyes became less placid.

"Against yourself, sir! And against the country!" The girl shivered; her hands, reddened by kitchen toil, were clasped fiercely against her breast. "There are many in it—even some among your bodyguard."

"How do you know?" the General asked sternly.

"One came to the room of Master Forbes, the gunsmith. I brought them lemons and rum, then listened outside the door —long enough to learn what is intended. Perhaps I shouldn't have, but . . . but they say about the tavern that Master Forbes is an agent of the British, swearing men for five guineas and the promise of land to turn traitor and serve King George!"

"Swearing them for what?"

"To take the city, sir, as soon as the ships from Boston get here. Some of the traitors are to break down the King's Bridge. Others, gathering at a tavern near the Upper Barracks, will shoot all the officers there, blow up the magazine, set the buildings afire. And you, sir, through the treachery of those among your bodyguard, are to be taken prisoner and either murdered or delivered over to the British to be hanged!"

The General, very calm, drew a sheet of paper toward him and took up a pen.

"Who are these men in my bodyguard?" he asked.

The girl's slim body quivered but she did not answer.

"You know their names?" Washington went on.

His visitor's only reply was an anguished nod.

For a long moment the General sat watching her closely. Then he gave an understanding sigh. A sweetheart involved, no doubt. Many, he thought, would give life for their country; this poor girl had the courage to give . . . love.

"I understand, my dear," he said gently, "and will not press you. After all, the names do not matter. It is enough that the plot is now discovered."

The girl sat staring at the floor, her body crumpled down like softened wax. Suddenly she raised her head, met the General's gaze with one as stern and resolute as his own.

"I accuse no one," she said, "for I am not sure. Let whoever is guilty suffer. One of my brothers has been killed, sir, serving with your army. I would gladly die myself, rather than see harm come to you, or to your cause. I have thought about this matter until my heart seems like to break, but beyond what I have told you I cannot speak. If a man I love has joined this plot he must pay for it. I could not care for one who was a traitor to his country." She rose, sweeping the tears from her eyes with a defiant gesture. "Now, sir, I must go. Should any learn that I came here and told you what I have, my life will be in danger. So I beg of you not to let the matter become known."

The General rose, very tall and straight behind his writing table, then stepped to the girl's side. Had he been addressing a princess his manner could not have been more courtly.

"You have honored me with your confidence, my dear," he said, taking her hand. "Rest assured I shall not break it." Smiling, he led her to the door. "Lieutenant," he went on to the officer on guard outside, "Give this young lady safe conduct beyond the garden, and see that no one speaks of her visit here, or attempts to learn her name; I do not wish her coming to be known. Then send a patrol to Corbie's tavern and take into custody the proprietor and a lodger named Forbes. Also place under arrest all members of my bodyguard who are off duty this evening. If Captain Mason is about, ask him to report to me at once."

From the edge of the garden Ellen ran across the meadows, hoping that Jim Bradford had not yet arrived. She had heard Forbes say, while standing outside the door, that Jim would return later. There might still be time to save him, before the patrol came. In her excitement she was not aware of the small, dark figure of Jasper, who, having followed her to Richmond Hill, was now racing ahead in a wide circle to gain the shadow of the trees that surrounded the tavern before she arrived.

Jim Bradford, having eaten a solitary supper, went back to Corbie's determined to find out, if possible, what devil's game this fellow Forbes was up to. In spite of the gunsmith's smooth assurances, Jim felt certain that some dangerous plot was afoot. Acres of fine farmland were not given away by the hundred for nothing. He would see Master Forbes, pretend to agree with him, draw the fellow out. . . .

He approached the tavern warily, going toward the side door, hoping thus to come upon Ellen, to have a word with her to remedy their quarrel at the well. She would be out walking with Tom Hickey later; if he could see her first. . . .

Then, to his surprise, she was at his side, white-faced and breathless, clutching his arm, uttering a fierce cry of warning.

"Jim! Don't go in!"

The young soldier stared down at her in amazement.

"Why not?" he asked.

"It . . . it would be folly . . . to . . . to listen to what Forbes has to say . . . take his bounty. . . ."

"But . . . why should you suppose . . . ?"

"Jim! I heard him tell Corbie you were coming. They've already got Tom Hickey . . . made him swear. . . ."

"That renegade! I'm not surprised to learn he's turned traitor! So you think that I. . . ." Jim Bradford laughed harshly, shaking her hand from his arm. "Thanks for the com-pliment, but I know what I'm about." He moved toward the door, but again the girl stopped him, shaking with terror.

"For God's sake get away, Jim . . . and quickly," she moaned. "Soldiers are coming! From Richmond Hill! To arrest everyone!"

Before she could finish, rapid footsteps, shouts of alarm sounded from within the tavern. The word brought by Jasper had sent the rats scurrying. Jim gave a snort of disgust.

"So you've warned Hickey and the others, have you?" he exclaimed, and turning, burst open the tavern door.

The hallway beyond was ill-lighted, but Jim made out the figure of Tom Hickey running down the stairs, with Master Forbes pounding desperately along behind him. At the far end of the hall he caught a glimpse of Corbie being helped through a rear window by his mulatto boy Jasper.

There was no time to see more, for now Hickey, racing to-ward the door, was upon him.

Jim Bradford met the Irishman's onslaught, fists flailing; in a moment the two men were locked in furious combat. Hickey

was quicker, but Jim had the advantage in both height and
weight. From side to side of the narrow hall the battle raged,
demolishing a chair, upsetting a small tilt-top table that stood
near the door. At last, with a fierce blow to the face, Jim sent
his opponent crashing to the floor amidst the remains of the
splintered chair.

Hickey, however, was by no means beaten. With an oath he
sprang to his feet, clutching a broken chair leg; before Jim
realized his danger the furious Irishman had brought the
weapon down upon his head. He sank to the floor, unconscious,
and Tom Hickey, hurdling his body, dashed through the open
door—and straight into the arms of the patrol which had just
arrived from Richmond Hill!

Ellen, gazing terrified at Jim's inert and silent figure, wondered if he had given his life to prevent the traitor's escape.

Jim Bradford, staring through a mist of pain, saw an elderly,
gray-haired man bending over him.

"Where am I?" he muttered. "And what happened?"

"You are in bed," the gray-haired man replied, "and have
been for many days, with a fractured skull. General Washington himself has come in person to inquire after you. Now,
however, you are mending rapidly. I am Dr. Murray."

Jim felt the heavy bandages that swathed his head. Things
seemed unreal; his mind was still bewildered.

"And Corbie . . . Forbes . . . Hickey?" he whispered.
"What of them?"

"Forbes got clean away to the ship. Corbie and his mulatto servant are believed to be in hiding somewhere near the city. Hickey, after almost killing you, leaped through the side door of the tavern into the hands of the soldiers sent to arrest him. But for you he would have had time to escape. The fellow, tried before a court martial, confessed his guilt and was hanged yesterday in the Bouwerie. Three brigades of troops with fixed bayonets accompanied him to the gallows, and twenty thousand persons assembled to witness his execution. So perish all traitors, say I."

"And the plot against General Washington?"

"That was completely overcome. Besides Hickey, two score of those involved, including the Mayor, have been taken into custody. They say, about town, that the General was warned of his danger by an unknown woman, but the story has not been confirmed." The doctor turned as a knock sounded at the door.

"For just a moment, my dear," Jim heard him say. "Someone to see you, Mr. Bradford."

Jim looked up. A white-faced girl came to the bedside, began to smooth his throbbing forehead.

"Ellen, darling," he whispered, pressing her small, cool hand.

"Jim!"

Unmindful of the doctor she bent down and kissed him.

As my torch blazed ever more brightly across the ocean, I watched the men of unhappy France turn to its guiding flame.

At first but slowly, blindly, with some disputing for weeks over futile theories while others in their rage tore down the Bastille.

Unlike the sturdy tradesmen and farmers of the New World, fighting the unjust taxation of a foreign-born king, I saw here in Paris mobs of half-starved peasants, ignorant serfs, knowing nothing of true democracy but filled with just and vengeful anger against a soulless nobility, a vicious and idle court. Beneath their rags lay the scars of bitter lashes. They cried out for justice, and sought it in blood. If they erred, then the blame lay less at their door than at the doors of those in high places who had permitted such conditions to exist. Cruel and thoughtless rulers who, sowing the wind of injustice and oppression, now reaped the whirlwind.

In horror I looked on while the streets of Paris ran red. Yet

I knew in my heart that it was not the real men of France who were responsible for this reign of terror, but a furious, half-crazed mob. This was not liberty, not democracy, as I had seen it across the water, but savage, unbridled license.

Soon the sober, sane citizens of France came to the rescue of their country. An unknown officer of the Army of the Rhine set down on paper the words and music of an immortal song. An unknown corporal of artillery emerged from the confusion to become France's greatest leader. The song was The Marseillaise, which has stirred the hearts of more liberty-loving men and women than any other anthem ever written. The leader was Napoleon Bonaparte, a military genius. Under his command, chanting the words of their inspiring song, the citizen-soldiers of France marched to glorious victory over the armies of Europe's self-anointed Kings.

I watched these citizens of the new Republic with a proud heart, knowing they fought for liberty, for democracy.

"MARCH ON—MARCH ON!"

THE young French officer who came to the door of M. Gison's house that afternoon was slim and smart in his captain's uniform, but his manner was troubled, and over his brilliant dark eyes hovered a dissatisfied frown.

The April day was fine, with clear spring sunshine lighting up the gray stone buildings and the tender young green of the linden trees. However, Rouget de l'Isle, of the Army of the Rhine, did not care particularly for Strassbourg, although he had been stationed in the busy Alsatian city for the past six months. Its people, he thought, were less joyous and open-hearted than those of his native hills and valleys of the Jura.

M. Gison, the music teacher, seemed different. Perhaps this was because Rouget, although a captain of engineers, had himself in his youth dreamed of following a musical career. That was before his father's insistence had forced him into the army. Now, with bridges and fortifications occupying time that might have been devoted to *chansons* and *ballades*, the young officer found in his frequent visits to the music master's home a pleasant relief from the rather dull atmosphere of the barracks. M. Gison being a widower, his daughter Suzanne kept house for him. She had an excellent soprano voice and dreamed of becoming an opera singer. The three of them spent many a delightful hour gathered about the master's fine English harpsichord.

This, however, was not the only reason that drove Rouget to seek the older man's companionship; they were both deeply interested in politics. When not discussing music, or listening to Suzanne sing, the two indulged in frequent and heated arguments upon such subjects as liberty, fraternity, and the rights of the common man. France was in a state of political ferment during those final and significant years of the eighteenth century, with men everywhere asking each other questions they had feared to ask before. Had not England fought for and maintained parliamentary rule, at the cost of the life of a king? Had not the men of the Low Countries gained their independence, set up a strong, free republic? Were the Swiss not at last rid of the Austrian yoke? Did not events, even across the seas, show that those who believed in liberty and possessed the neces-

sary courage to fight, might obtain it? What right had kings
to rule, compared with the right of free men to govern themselves? Throughout the entire civilized world such questions
were being asked and answered, yet in France a stupid monarch
and his corrupt and vicious court still squandered on frivolities
the taxes wrung from a starving people, while a National Assembly in Paris debated furiously what had best be done. To
Rouget de l'Isle the answers seemed simple. The Jura region
from whence he came bordered on Switzerland . . . he had
been brought up in an atmosphere of freedom common to men
who breathed the high, clear air of mountain peaks. However,
M. Gison, a native of the Rhine valley, did not always agree;
their arguments, while good-natured, were often violent.

The music teacher's servant, a gray-haired Alsatian woman,
opened the door in answer to Rouget's knocks.

"Ah . . . *Monsieur le Capitaine!*" she exclaimed, smiling.
"You wish to see the master? He has gone to the chemist's
shop with Mlle. Suzanne, to take the sunshine, and buy a package of snuff. But you will enter, will you not, and wait? They
will return soon, I am sure."

Rouget stepped into the narrow, somewhat gloomy hall,
went down it to a large, square room overlooking the garden.
This was M. Gison's *atelier*, his studio, in which from nine to
four each day he gave his pupils lessons on the harpsichord.
Now, with the afternoon nearly over, it was deserted.

Still frowning, Rouget sat down before the handsome instru-
ment, ran his fingers lovingly along its ivory keys. In spite of

his uniform, the eager, youthful lines of his face suggested the
musician rather than the soldier.

There was something about a pianoforte that always impelled
him to play. A fragment of melody had been haunting his
mind for days . . . the opening bars of some dimly remembered folk song, perhaps, heard as a child . . . but try as he
would, the simple air would not come back to him. Chord
after chord echoed through the room, with tripping sequences
of notes between, but in the end Rouget, defeated, brought
both hands down on the keys with a resounding crash.

A chuckle from the doorway caused him to turn. M. Gison
stood in it, smiling. The music master's flowing gray hair, his
huge, well-fed body and broad red face made him an imposing
figure, especially in the eyes of his youthful and timid pupils.

"So!" he grunted, smiling. "While I am away, you would
break my poor harpsichord to pieces! *Sacre bleu!*"

"Pardon!" Rouget sprang up. "For a week I have tried, but
the air still escapes me."

"What air, my son?" The music master sank into a shabby,
leather-covered chair.

"Something I seem to remember from my childhood, yet
when I try to play it, the melody will not come. Like a song
heard in a dream. . . ."

M. Gison opened the small package he held in his hands and
poured snuff into a battered silver box.

"Many famous composers, I am told," he said with vast
gravity, "have worked in that way. A fragment of melody,

which they seem to have heard before, haunting, tormenting them . . . yet in the end turning out to be no memory at all, but a new and original air. Keep after it, my boy. Who knows? Some day it may come to you in the twinkling of an eye, and —*voila!* You give to the world a great masterpiece!"

Rouget reddened a little under the old musician's irony. The few minor songs he had written in Suzanne's honor scarcely entitled him to rank as a famous composer. He managed, however, to laugh.

"But why should you worry yourself over this forgotten melody?" the music master went on. "Are you trying to write a new song? For a new sweetheart, perhaps?"

"Yes," Rouget said steadily. "A new song. But not for any sweetheart. For France."

"Eh!" M. Gison spilled the pinch of snuff he was on the point of taking. "What do you mean? France has plenty of songs."

"Too many!" Rouget exclaimed, brushing the dark hair back from his forehead. "Madrigals, love serenades, drinking songs, dances! Songs filled with joy, gaiety, laughter! But now is no time for men to laugh! We face serious days! Now France must march!"

"So you would write us a marching song, eh?"

"If I could," Rouget muttered. "If I only could. Sometimes the air seems so near that it rings like a bugle call in my ears. Yet whenever I try to grasp it. . . ." He shook his head despairingly.

M. Gison closed his snuffbox with a click. "You think, then," he asked harshly, "that a song would help those madmen now gathered in Paris?"

"Why not, if it were strong and fine enough to stir, to inspire them! Also, my friend, why do you call the members of the National Assembly madmen?"

The music master did not at once reply. For several moments he sat gazing through one of the windows facing the garden. When he spoke his voice was dry, precise.

"As you know, M. de l'Isle," he said, "I am a believer in liberty, in democracy. History has shown us that only when men are free can they rise to the full height of their genius. But this thing we call freedom is not to be given to everyone. As well offer a rare vintage wine to the mob. They would not appreciate it."

"Then you do not believe in government by the people?" Rouget said quickly.

"Not by all the people, certainly. Even in democratic Greece only the intelligent classes ruled. Athens had her slaves, her serfs, as France has. Give the peasants justice, by all means, but not freedom; they would only abuse it."

Rouget de l'Isle shook his head.

"You are wrong, Master," he objected. "There are no slaves in the Low Countries, in Switzerland. There all men are free."

"That is perhaps because their peoples are intelligent, educated, fit to enjoy freedom. In France things are different. Behold the present madness in Paris. Mobs roaming the streets,

threatening death to the nobles, the clergy, even the King. Demanding that great estates be divided. Bloodthirsty mobs, seeking liberty, to do what? To rob, to murder their betters! Is it
for such *canaille* you would write an invitation to march?"

"No!" Rouget exclaimed hotly. "Do not blame all France
for what is going on in Paris! Rather blame those who have
created such conditions. For years, in our unhappy country,
the peasants have been beaten, starved, robbed by cruel and
indifferent masters! Sold like cattle, along with the lands they
are forced to till. Do you wonder that, remembering their rags,
their lashes, these unfortunates cry out for revenge? But this
mob of extremists is not France. All over the land are sober,
thinking men like you or me—earnest men—doctors, shopkeepers, artisans, merchants, soldiers, farmers, who are the real
strength of the nation. It is to those I would appeal. They must
act, and promptly, if the wrongs of the people are to be righted
and France is once more to be great. Without them this uprising in Paris will come to nothing. The Prussians, the Austrians
will step in, the ringleaders of the movement will be executed
and all will continue as before." Rouget de l'Isle bent over the
keys of the harpsichord, struck a few random notes. "Nothing," he went on, "so stirs the hearts of a people as a patriotic
anthem. It has been my dream to write one . . . a song to
which all liberty-loving Frenchmen might march. But it remains
a dream, and no more." He sank dejectedly into a chair.

M. Gison pulled the bell cord at his elbow. "Perhaps a glass
of wine may inspire you," he said drily. "Ah . . . Suzanne,"

he went on, as his daughter came down the hall. "Tell Paula
to bring us a bottle of Moselle. . . . And then come and
greet our young captain of engineers, M. de l'Isle; he is writing
a new song."

Rouget bent low over the girl's slim fingers.

"Only trying to, *mademoiselle*," he murmured.

"To me?" Suzanne asked, smiling.

"No," her father broke in. "To France. He is ambitious.
Instead of appealing to the love of one woman, he plans to in-
flame the heart of an entire nation."

Suzanne joined in her father's laughter; she liked the young
officer, but was not at all in love with him.

"Captain de l'Isle is wise not to write love songs to me,
since he knows I am devoted only to my art. But one favor,
monsieur, I will ask." She turned quickly to Rouget. "When
this masterpiece of yours is finished, grant me the honor of
being the first to sing it in public."

"Gladly," Rouget agreed. "I could not hope, *mademoiselle*,
to find a more charming sponsor."

"Here is our wine," M. Gison exclaimed, as Paula appeared
with the bottle. "Let us drink, *Monsieur le Capitaine*, to this
unborn child of your genius!" Laughing, he filled the three
glasses.

All the way back to the barracks Rouget de l'Isle thought
of his song. Even though M. Gison and Suzanne had made
a joke of it, the idea persisted. Other nations had their great
national airs . . . why not France?

At the officers' mess he found a visitor—a tanned and bearded man who was introduced as Captain Leroux. Clear-eyed and quick of movement, he suggested at once the *voya-geur,* the traveler.

"Leroux is a native of Strassbourg," one of Rouget's brother officers explained. "He was overseas with the Marquis de Lafayette, and has just come from Paris. Our Colonel has in-vited him to supper."

"I hope he will tell us something of the revolution in Amer-ica," Rouget said; "and how the people there won freedom from the English."

Captain Leroux, when the simple meal had been eaten and the coffee passed around, was ready and indeed eager to talk of his experiences overseas.

"That is vast and noble country across the water," he said, "where all men are now declared to be equal. . . ."

"But, *monsieur,*" a young lieutenant asked, "how is it pos-sible to make men equal, merely by declaring them so? Could we, here in France, by passing laws, make a lackey the equal of a marquis, a peasant the equal of a king?"

Captain Leroux nodded, his eyes glowing.

"Why not?" he replied. "They are equal before God. But you mistake the meaning of that new democracy. It proclaims only that all men are created equal, so that none may start life as either king or peasant by reason of accident of birth. Thus all begin as free men. Free by reason of their ability, their industry and courage, to make themselves what they will. In

that great country, where after the war's end I traveled much,
I found the smith who shod my horse as proud as I, since he
knew that by his labor and energy he might presently ride a
horse of his own. In a land where none need bow to his neighbor, all can hold their heads high. The farmer at his plow, the
merchant in his counting house, the artisan in his shop, the
village lad on his way to school—each may nurse in his heart
a cherished dream, knowing himself free to make it come true.
That, my friends, is liberty. That is democracy. The right to
live one's dreams. From what I have seen of the new states
of America, I predict for them a glorious future. Freedom is,
after all, not a material thing to hold in one's hand like wealth,
or land, or title. It is a possession of the spirit—a state of mind,
of heart. With it, the poorest laborer may sing. Without it,
even princes go about in fear and trembling."

"And did you find that spirit in Paris?" one of the younger
officers asked. "The true spirit of liberty, of democracy?"

Captain Leroux put down his wineglass, frowning.

"It is there, certainly," he said. "But with it goes a dangerous and terrible desire for revenge. In America no such desire
was present. The colonists who crossed the ocean were already
free and independent men. Here in France the revolution is
passing into the hands of a low and ignorant rabble, who see
in freedom only an opportunity to murder those who have
oppressed them, to appropriate their wealth. Just before I left
Paris, General de Lafayette presented to the Assembly a state-
ment of the people's demands, drawn up along the lines of the

American Declaration of Independence. It was voted down as being too conservative. The Paris mob wants blood. Its leaders, in their mad desire to sweep aside all classes, have even begun to turn against Lafayette, calling him a traitor to the people! I am a Frenchman, *messieurs*. I believe in the future of France. Like Lafayette, I am in favor of freedom, of democ-racy. I hope to see established in this country a republican form of government such as now exists in America. But it must be the work of sober, thinking men, not of extremists leading a bloodthirsty rabble. The real people of France must come for-ward, take part in the struggle, lend a hand to the great task. Men of courage, of vision. Only thus can our country be saved from the terrors of anarchy—or from defeat by our foes!"

A sudden silence fell about the table. In spite of the course of events in Paris, it was a dangerous matter for an officer of the army to express such revolutionary sentiments. Although the Bastille had been torn down, the King still ruled. Captain Leroux, however, did not seem afraid. He sprang to his feet, raised his wineglass.

"Officers of the Army of the Rhine!" he cried. "Soldiers of France! I stand with General Lafayette! If he is a traitor to his country, then so am I! But meanwhile, do not forget that ene-mies, powerful enemies, threaten us from beyond our borders. Nations sworn to defend the divine rights of kings. Arouse yourselves! To arms! For your country, your Fatherland! In the name of freedom! Form your ranks! March on! Long live France!"

The captain drained his glass, hurled it crashing to the floor. The officers about the table, rising to their feet, did likewise. The messroom resounded with their cheers.

Rouget de l'Isle sank back into his chair, his eyes glowing. He had been deeply moved by Captain Leroux's toast. Those were the sentiments, the words he sought. Words to arouse emotion, to set the hearts of his countrymen aflame. Simple, direct words, that all could understand. If only he could find an equally simple and inspiring air. He scarcely listened as Leroux went on to tell of the fighting in America, of the un-trained farmer boys facing seasoned veterans, of long years of discouragement, and of final victory at a place called York-town, where he had seen the British general Cornwallis sur-render his sword, while his vanquished army marched between long lines of French and American troops. Soldiers of France, he said, had fought for liberty across an ocean—why should they not fight for it with equal valor and determination here at home?

In the midst of the discussion Rouget hurried to his room. He was eager to set down the simple words that had so thrilled him, arrange them in a form to be sung. "March on . . . march on! . . . Form your battalions! To arms! Defend the Fatherland! Sons of France!" But although a rude chorus took shape in his mind, no appropriate air came with it, in spite of the endless notes he set down. All the musical phrases he was able to create seemed either commonplace jingles, or heavy, ponderous airs more suited to solemn church processions than to an inspiring military march. Discouraged, he threw himself across the bed.

The night was quiet, so that small, unimportant sounds could be plainly heard. Dogs barking. The distant rumble of a cart as its wheels passed over the cobblestones. A woman singing in a nearby house. Churchbells announcing the hour. The tramp of men in the barrack yard as sentries were relieved. Soldiers' voices raised in shrill argument over a game of dice.

Rouget closed his eyes, lay for a few moments half awake. The clear, sweet notes of a bugle came to him, apparently from somewhere nearby. A member of the regimental band, no doubt, practising his military calls. The charge. The retreat. To arms! Over and over, at times almost in the room, at others, faint and far off. Between the high, clear notes Rouget seemed to hear the muffled footsteps of marching men. He rubbed his eyes, lay still, wondering if he had been asleep. No men would be marching at this hour.

Suddenly, as though tired of sounding the same calls over and over, the bugler broke into another, almost triumphant air. A swift musical passage that might have been mere extemporizing, or perhaps the opening bars of some long-forgotten mountaineers' call.

For a breathless moment the notes hung like golden stars in the darkness, then died away. But during that moment there had been unlocked in Rouget's brain a long-closed door.

With a cry of joy he leaped from the bed, seized paper and pen. How easily the stirring melody came, now that the magic key to inspiration had been found. He wrote the notes down with scarcely a change, scrawling swift passionate words beneath them. Inside of an hour he was pounding frantically at M. Gison's door.

"Open! Open!" he cried.

The music master, yawning, shuffled down the hall.

"Who knocks?" he asked, peering into the gloom about the doorway.

"It is I—Rouget de l'Isle."

"Well . . . what do you want?" M. Gison had been dozing, and objected to being aroused in this sudden and violent fashion.

"I've found it, Master! I've found it!" Rouget exclaimed, waving the sheet of paper under the music teacher's nose. Trembling with excitement he stepped into the hall.

"Found what?"

"The air for my new song!"

"Eh? Well . . . come in . . . come in." M. Gison led the way to his *atelier*. "Although why all this excitement over a musical composition, when most persons are thinking of bed. . . ."

"Wait until you hear it, Master! Then you will understand! I ran all the way!" Rouget flung himself on the bench before the harpsichord, propped the sheet of paper against the music rack. "Listen!" He struck a resounding note, began to play.

M. Gison, leaning with half-closed eyes against the back of his chair, suddenly opened them, sat up, as the simple but inspiring strains swept through the room. When Rouget came to the chorus, he sang aloud,

> "To arms! to arms! ye brave!
> The avenging sword unsheath!
> March on! March on! all hearts resolved
> On victory, or death!"

Stout as M. Gison was, the words, the music lifted him out of his chair, drew him to Rouget's side.

"*Sacré nom!*" he cried. "You have indeed found it, my boy! Magnificent, without doubt! A triumph! A masterpiece!"

"I'm not sure," Rouget went on, flushing beneath such extravagant praise, "whether it came to me in a dream, or was something I heard a bugler play. . . ."

"Nonsense . . . nonsense, my boy!" The Master waved such considerations aside as though they were of no importance. "All composers have such moments of inspiration."

Suzanne, hurrying downstairs from the floor above, burst into the studio.

"M. de l'Isle!" she cried. "Is that air I have just heard you play your new composition?"

"Yes, *mademoiselle*. My song to France. Although at present I am calling it the Chant of the Army of the Rhine."

Suzanne snatched the sheet of paper from the music rack, glancing over the hastily penned words.

"Play!" she commanded, waving toward the harpsichord, "that I may have the honor of being the first to sing it."

Onward marched the men of Marseilles, singing their new
battle song.

Rouget struck the keys. The girl's clear soprano voice was like a bugle call, piercing the evening stillness. As she finished, it rose in a triumphant crescendo.

M. Gison applauded boisterously. Paula, the maid, stood gaping in the narrow hall. Knocks sounded at the door as neighbors came to ask the name of the song they had just listened to. Suzanne was begged to sing it again, that the words might be more clearly heard.

She did so, with the front door of the house open, and a group of listeners standing in the street outside. When she had finished, people went away, humming, whistling the brave, unforgettable air.

"*Monsieur le Capitaine,*" the music master said impressively, "you have composed the finest military march it has ever been my good fortune to hear! I predict that before a week has passed the whole town will be singing it. Congratulations, my boy! We must celebrate the occasion over a bottle of champagne!"

M. Gison was right. Within a week the song had obtained such popularity that Rouget was called upon to sing it at a banquet given by the Mayor. But it was not until several months had passed that the stirring air received its present name, and became the battlecry of the French Republic.

As Rouget de l'Isle had hoped and predicted, people all over the country now began to take a hand in the movement for freedom, until then largely confined to Paris.

Early in July the municipality of Marseilles, on the Mediterranean coast, brought together a company of artisans, sailors, shopkeepers—men who, in the words of their leader, Barba-roux, "knew how to die." Carrying swords and muskets, assembled in military formation with captains of tens and fifties, taking with them even some small cannon, they set out for Paris, with Rouget de l'Isle's new song on their lips. No longer the Chant of the Army of the Rhine, now, but the Song of the Marseillaise—the song of a new and triumphant France!

This column of grave and determined men, marching shoulder to shoulder across country, wore liberty caps on their heads and nursed the vision of a new and glorious freedom in their hearts. Through strange villages and towns and cities they went, "toward an unknown destiny," yet with a purpose that would not be denied. Simple householders, who had laid aside their tools, abandoned their crafts, to march six hundred miles in order to strike down the tyrant, as Rouget de l'Isle's stirring words urged them to do. Not a mob of vengeful peasants and serfs, seeking through hate to rob and murder their aristocratic and titled masters, but sturdy, honest men who believed that justice and freedom were inalienable rights of every citizen, and were ready, if necessary, to die for their cause. Onward they marched, singing their new battle song . . . vanguard of the great Army of the People which was soon to defeat the Prussian invaders on the Field of Valmy, and carry the Tricolor of France, the banner of Liberty, Equality and Fraternity, to glorious victory over all the crowned heads of Europe.

In Greece, in Rome, in the city-states of Italy, I had watched men fight with supreme courage to gain their freedom, only to sacrifice it, when victory had been won, upon the altar of a Conqueror's ambitions.

Now in France I saw the same sorry drama enacted. There, too, the brave ideals of Liberty, Equality and Fraternity were to be tossed aside to please the vanity of a Corsican adventurer. The men of Valmy, of Austerlitz, had not learned that great as is the courage needed to gain liberty, even greater courage may be required in order to preserve it. Like Alexander, like Caesar, Napoleon Bonaparte was a master of war. To him, the hopes and ideals of the French people meant nothing. His ambition was to found, not a Republic, but an Empire, a dynasty. His greatest wish was to see his descendants rule the continent of Europe, and in pursuit of that small vanity he led France to defeat at Waterloo. Little had it profited a struggling people, to throw aside a worthless King and gain a tinseled Emperor. As I watched the Old Guard die, I began to despair of the future of Man. Was he always to win the victory, only to toss it aside in his hour of triumph?

Even in the great new democracy of the West, now rising to power beyond the ocean, I saw signs of this evil tendency appear. Scarcely had the wounds of Revolution healed, when cunning and ambitious men sought to forge fresh chains with which to bind the liberties of the people. *Failing in their efforts to make George Washington a king, they began to hedge the presidency about with the prerogatives of royalty. Laws were passed making it a felony to criticize those in public office or to disagree with the acts of the government. Were the American people also to be robbed of those vital bulwarks of liberty, freedom of speech, freedom of the press? Already men were being imprisoned by the score for having dared to speak their minds as free citizens of the Republic! In fear and anger I looked on, knowing how swiftly and surely that road would lead to disaster. When the voice of the people is stilled there remains but a step to dictatorship and enslavement of the nation.*

Then I saw a great statesman rise, to take up the fight for democracy. Thomas Jefferson, author of the Declaration of Independence, who had not only the wisdom to see the danger in which his country stood, but the courage to combat it. He knew that the War of the Revolution had given liberty to the American people, and he was determined that the fruits of victory should be preserved.

I rejoiced as the battle lines were drawn, hoping that here in this brave new land men would at last have vision to see and follow the road my torch so clearly pointed out . . . the road to true democracy!

VOX POPULI

Tom Knox came into the house that winter afternoon, his face and hands red from the cold. He stood for a while with his back to the kitchen fire, watching his mother set the table for supper.

"Begun to snow?" she asked, glancing through the frosted window panes.

"Yes." Tom brushed some flakes from his sleeve. "How's Dad feeling? Better?"

"Yes. Long as he stays indoors this kind of weather."

Sam Knox came into the room, coughing. His tall frame was bent a little, his cheeks were thin and sunken. A bullet through the chest while serving with General Washington's army had weakened his lungs.

"That heifer back on her feed, son?" he asked.

"Yes. I gave her a hot bran mash. Don't worry, Dad; I'll look after everything. Jud Crothers stopped by a while ago on his way back from town—said he'd be over tonight for a talk—politics."

"H·m·m. Jud's a fire·eater, sure enough." Mr. Knox chuckled. "The way he pitches into President Adams and the Congress. What's he up to now—running for town council?"

Tom laughed, but the look in his eyes was serious.

"Jud's not looking for office, Dad," he said gravely. "It's democracy he's preaching, freedom of speech and the press. He says Hamilton and his Federalists are out to destroy them. From what I can see, he's right. Jud gets around, selling his produce to the New Brunswick tavern keepers. Hears what people traveling north and south by the post road have to say. Picks up the latest news. He claims he has something special for us, tonight."

"Maybe." Sam Knox frowned. "Just the same I don't like the way Jud talks about the administration and the govern· ment. John Adams is a good man, a good president."

"It's not Mr. Adams that Jud's so bitter against, Dad, but the men around him, his cabinet. Pickering, Wolcott, McHenry. All dyed·in·the·wool Federalists, taking their orders from Alex· ander Hamilton. And everybody knows Mr. Hamilton despises the common people. That's the crowd who put over the Anti· alien and Sedition Acts—they and their friends in the Con· gress."

"Seems like you're getting to be quite a politician yourself, Son. Don't let Jud Crothers and his ideas run away with you; he's a pretty wild talker at times."

"I've been studying these questions on my own account, Dad!" Tom replied, his face suddenly flushing. "And as far as I can see, this Sedition Act is against the Constitution. Mr. Jefferson thinks so. The Virginia and Kentucky legislatures have condemned it. You see, Jud brings me newspapers. I've been reading them. That's how I know."

"What's there about this Sedition Act to get you so excited? Some say it's a good thing."

"The Federalists think so, of course. They don't believe the people have any rights. Do you know that that Act makes it a crime to speak, write, print, or publish anything against the government?"

Mrs. Knox, slicing a loaf of bread, looked up.

"Seems to me that's a very good law, Tom," she said. "We can't have people criticizing Congress and the President."

"Why not? Don't you know, Mother, that freedom of speech, of the press, are guaranteed under the Bill of Rights in the Constitution? That's what Dad fought for, the right of every man to come out and say what he thinks in public. That's democracy. If you take free speech away, we might just as well have a king and be done with it!"

Mrs. Knox smiled placidly, sat down at the table.

"Supper's ready," she said. "You can talk politics after you've et. I hope Jud Crothers won't get you into any trouble, with your father needing you to look after things while he's ailing."

The supper dishes had been cleared away when Jud Crothers arrived, stamping the snow from his boots. He greeted the others noisily, hung his greatcoat behind the kitchen door, and sat down at the fire.

"Snow's still falling, folks," he said, warming his hands before the cheerful blaze. "Hope it lets up, on account of tomorrow's parade."

"What parade?" Sam Knox asked.

"I came over to tell you." Jud Crothers' eyes were as bright as new pennies. "Ever hear of Matthew Lyon, Sam?"

"Can't say as I have." Mr. Knox shook his head.

"Would, effen you'd read the newspapers oftener. Anyway, Matt Lyon's a member of Congress, from Vermont. A good Democrat, publishes a paper up in Rutland, where he lives. The Federalists don't like him because he isn't afraid to speak his mind. Seems he printed a letter in his newspaper a while ago, saying the President's address to Congress was a 'bullying speech' and the Senate's reply to it 'stupid.' Well, folks, just for that he was dragged into court, found guilty under the Sedition Act and sentenced to four months in prison with a fine of one thousand dollars to boot! Think of it! Jailing a good American citizen, a member of Congress, for daring to criticize his masters! King George himself wouldn't have done as much! And they call this a free country! Looks to me like we're just a lot of slaves!"

"We don't have to be!" Tom muttered. "The Constitution says. . . ."

"Wait a minute!" The little man went on, his face red as a turkey cock's. "I haven't told you all. Instead of putting Matt Lyon in jail in Rutland, like they should've, the marshal carried him off to a dirty little hole called Vergennes. Set him on a horse and rode him forty miles across country with a pistol at his back. Wouldn't even let him go home to fetch his books and papers. Threw him into a filthy hogpen of a cell kept especially for felons of the worst type, a place you could hardly turn 'round in, with no way to heat it; so Matt had to sit and shiver day and night, wrapped up in his greatcoat. Refused to let him have even pen and paper. It makes my blood boil just to think of it! We might as well be living in Rooshia!"

"The poor man," Mrs. Knox murmured. "Didn't his friends do anything to help him?"

"Yes, Mrs. Knox," Crothers said, sputtering. "The farmers in Vermont—the Green Mountain Boys that had fought along with Lyon during the War, under Colonel Ethan Allen—got together and marched to Vergennes in a body, threatening to tear the jail down! And what do you think this wicked and seditious criminal said to them? Through the bars of his cage! He told those Vermont boys to avoid all violence and seek redress at the polls! That's the sort of a man Matt Lyon is! An honest citizen and good Democrat. So his friends took his advice, signed a petition, sent it off to President Adams. And that high and mighty gentleman refused to receive it! Then the

Set him on a horse and rode him forty miles with a pistol
at his back.

Vermonters got up on their hind legs and reëlected Matt to Congress, while he was shivering in his dirty little cell! I take off my hat to them. But those Federalists down in Philadelphia weren't through yet. Knowing a poor editor like Matt Lyon didn't have a thousand dollars or any part of it, they refused to let him take his seat in Congress until he'd paid his fine! I tell you, folks, if this sort of thing is what we fought the Revolution for, we may have to fight another one!"

"Couldn't his friends raise the money?" Tom asked, his eyes blazing.

"They're poor folks, like us, son, and a thousand dollars don't grow on every tree. But he got help. From men like Tom Jefferson, and others—Mr. Gallatin, Mr. Madison—real men, not time-serving politicians. Senator Mason of Virginia rode into that little town of Vergennes with a thousand dollars, gold, in his saddlebags! And met another good Democrat, a Vermonter named Austen, at the door of the jail carrying as much more, in silver! A fellow who stopped at Drake's tavern in Brunswick last week was up there in Vermont at the time and saw it. He says when Lyon came out of his cell there were thousands of people waiting to cheer him. And when he announced he was going to Philadelphia, to take his seat in Congress, they put him and his wife in a sleigh and started him off with a big procession, soldiers marching, school children singing, bands playing, flags waving—a regular parade! Same thing all the way down through New York. Crowds out to cheer him. . . . Now here's why I came over this evening.

Matthew Lyon is due to pass through New Brunswick around noon tomorrow. His party was to sleep at Newark tonight, one of the stagecoach drivers said. So I want you, Sam, and Tom to come in town tomorrow and help give Mr. Lyon the sort of reception he deserves."

"I'm afraid Sam can't, Jud," Mrs. Knox said. "With his cough, he hadn't ought to be standing around in the cold." She overrode her husband's protests gently. "No, Sam. Tom can go."

Jud Crothers, in spite of his disappointment, nodded.

"Reckon you're right, ma'am," he said. "The boys, most of 'em old soldiers, figure to meet Mr. Lyon at the bridge, with a fife and drum corps, welcoming him with a little speech—I'm supposed to do that—and escort his party through town. Brunswick is full of Federalists. They might start throwing snowballs, or rocks. So we thought all good friends of democracy and Thomas Jefferson ought to turn out."

"I'll be there, Mr. Crothers!" Tom said. "What time are you leaving for town?"

"Around nine. Have to take a passel of ducks to Mr. Vernon. You come on over, drive in with me. And you might bring your dad's flintlock with you, long as he can't come himself."

Sam Knox glanced at the musket hanging from two pegs across the chimney breast.

"Reckon Tom won't be needing a gun, Jud," he said. "Don't forget what Mr. Lyon told the Green Mountain Boys about not using violence and settling things at the polls. Tom's got his fists, in case any trouble comes up. That flintlock stays where it is."

Jud Crothers sprang to his feet, chuckling.

"All the boys figured to do, Sam, was fire a military salute," he said. "See you tomorrow, Tom. Good night, folks." He strode off, whistling "The Liberty Tree."

Tom reached the house next morning to find the little man loading crates of ducks into his battered one-horse sleigh. The snow had stopped toward midnight; the day was sunny and clear. By ten o'clock the crates had been delivered to Mr. Ver-non's tavern, and Jud drove his sleigh to a blacksmith's shop near the river, where he planned to leave it during the day.

Here a score of men in faded uniforms had already gathered, with others arriving momentarily. In the smithy yard, a dozen drummers and fifers were practicing military airs.

"They took Matt Lyon to jail playing the 'Rogue's March,'" Jud called to the musicians. "We'll escort him through town to the strains of 'Yankee Doodle'!"

In addition to the ex-soldiers, there were many younger men in the crowd about the shop, sons of neighboring farmers, most of whom Tom knew. He started to join them. Jud Crothers pointed to a stout cask, standing near the gate of the smithy.

"Take this down to the bridge, boys," he said. "I'll be along in a jiffy."

Tom and one of his friends rolled the empty cask down to the bridge, the others following. In a few moments Jud appeared, with a square piece of board under one arm, a hammer in his hand. Behind him were two men carrying a long, slender pole.

"Stand the cask on end here," he said, indicating a spot near the side of the road. "Set the pole up behind it."

In a few moments the stake had been driven into the ground, lashed firmly to the cask by a length of rope. Crothers, smiling broadly, climbed to the top of the cask and nailed the piece of board he carried to the pole. Painted on it in large black letters were the words, DOWN WITH FEDERALIST TYRANTS! NO STAMP TAX—NO SEDITION ACT. When Jud took a scarlet Liberty Cap from his pocket, set it on top of the pole, everyone cheered.

A lame veteran carrying a large American flag stationed himself in the center of the road, with the drummers and fifers behind him. The soldiers with their flintlocks lined up on either side of the roadway, ready to escort Mr. Lyon's sleigh as a guard of honor. Tom and the younger men stood around Jud Crothers, who was perched on top of his cask. Some distance away a group of Federalist sympathizers, distinguished by their more prosperous appearance, had gathered to watch the proceedings. From time to time they jeered lustily, hurling an occasional snowball at Jud's defiant sign.

Just before noon a man came riding over the bridge to announce that Mr. Lyon's sleigh was close at hand. In a few moments it appeared. Jud Crothers straightened his slim shoulders. The drummers and fifers began to play. The veterans along the roadside presented arms. Across the bridge came the hero of Vergennes, wrapped in a heavy coat, his wife at his side. Small flags decorated the front of the sleigh; there were red, white and blue cockades in the bridles of the horses.

Cheers from the crowd greeted Mr. Lyon's appearance. The drummers and fifers became more spirited. At the sight of Jud, standing on the cask, the sleigh came to a halt. The little man waved his hand for silence, then began to speak.

"In the name of the free men of New Brunswick," he cried, "I have the honor to welcome in our midst that distinguished patriot and defender of the people's liberties, that honest and fearless editor, that martyr to a stupid and tyrannical govern-ment, the Honorable Matthew Lyon of Vermont! May he con-tinue his good work until Alexander Hamilton and his Feder-alist cohorts are driven from the seats of the mighty, and Thomas Jefferson, friend of the people, is placed in the presi-dential chair. Hurrah for liberty! Hurrah for the freedom of the press. Hurrah for Matthew Lyon!"

The cheers of the crowd redoubled. The veterans fired their muskets in the air. Mr. Lyon rose from his seat, took off his hat and waved it.

"I appreciate this demonstration, friends," he said, "not as a tribute to me, but to the cause I represent—the cause of lib-erty and of democracy! The things we fought for in '76! I was arrested, thrown into jail like a common criminal, for pub-lishing an article in my newspaper criticizing the President and the government! Whether my criticisms were just or unjust is beside the question. What I am contending for . . . what we must all contend for if this is to remain a free country . . . was my right to express them! The right of every man to express his opinions, his views! Do you know that over a score of others have been similarly arrested, convicted, throughout the country? At least one has died, in Boston, as a result of ill treatment! Shall men be fined, thrown into jail for daring to speak their minds? Since when has that been a crime? Against such outrageous tyranny, my friends, every free man must be ready to fight!"

Ringing cheers from the youths about Jud Crothers' cask greeted his words, but the group of Federalists farther up the road responded with catcalls and jeers. A snowball thrown by one of them glanced off Mr. Lyon's shoulder, spattered his wife, sitting beside him in the sleigh. He bent down, brushing the snow from her cheeks.

"To such arguments," he said, smiling, "the best retort is silence." He signaled to the driver of the sleigh to go on.

The man carrying the flag raised his pole. The drum and fife corps struck up the lively strains of "Yankee Doodle." The escort of veterans, muskets over their shoulders, took their places at either side of the sleigh as it prepared to move off.

Glancing along the road, Tom saw that the crowd of Federalist sympathizers had grown larger. A number of older men, swarming from a nearby tavern, joined them, partly blocking the street. More snowballs, brickbats, rocks, began to fly, aimed mostly at Jud Crothers and at the Liberty Pole.

Tom and the young men with him had taken their places behind Matt Lyon's sleigh, meaning to escort it through the town. One of the Federalists pointed to the sign above Jud Crothers' head.

"Come on, boys!" he shouted. "Let's tear it down!"

As a new volley of missiles descended upon Jud, Tom sprang toward the cask.

"This way, fellows! We can't desert Jud!" he called out. "Don't let them get the pole; he's in the right!"

The Jeffersonians, some two score in all, hastily surrounded Jud's cask. At the same moment the Federalist party advanced in a rush. The driver of Mr. Lyon's sleigh, seeing he could not go forward while the road was blocked, turned into the ditch, climbed down to quiet the frightened horses. Jud Crothers, dancing about on his cask like a jumping jack as he sought to evade the shower of snowballs, shouted encouragement to his defenders.

"Give the rascals what they deserve!" he cried. "We want no tyrants here in America!"

Tom, in the forefront of the battle, fought desperately to keep the attackers back. A tall, well-dressed youth who seemed to be one of their leaders dashed toward the pole; Tom sent him sprawling with a well-aimed clout on the jaw. Two others, older men, sprang forward from either side. There was no time for the niceties of conflict; Tom tripped one of them up with a twist of his leg, butted the other in the stomach. A snowball, ice-hard, struck him on the cheek, making a deep gash; he

wiped off the blood with his coat-sleeve, turned to seize a fellow armed with a club about the waist and hurled him into
the ranks of his onrushing companions.

Heads were being cracked, noses bloodied, eyes blackened
on both sides. Three times the Federalists charged with increasing fury, but each time they were thrown back, leaving Jud
Crothers' cask and the Liberty Pole still intact. Groups of
townspeople, hearing the roar of the battle, came hurrying down
the road, still further blocking it. The Revolutionary veterans,
middle-aged men, stood muskets in hand about Mr. Lyon's
sleigh, trying to keep back the swirling crowd, while his coach-
man clung to the bridles of the excited horses. As for the members of the drum and fife corps, they tossed aside their instruments and ran headlong to the assistance of Tom and his party,
just in time to prevent the Liberty Pole from going down beneath sheer weight of numbers. To escape the shower of
flying missiles, Mrs. Lyon had buried her head in the folds of
a bearskin laprobe. Her husband stood beside her, grimly watching the conflict.

A sharp report caused Tom to turn his head. The battling
crowd froze to swift attention. Tom, brushing the sweat from
his eyes, peered along the street, suddenly apprehensive. If
someone in the crowd, drunk perhaps, had fired a musket, the
fight so harmlessly begun might end in bloodshed. Tempers
were high; he heard Jud Crothers shouting, saw him point.

The crowd had parted. Three men were advancing toward
the cask. One held a smoking pistol, its muzzle pointed sky-

ward. There was a glittering badge on the breast of his coat. The two men with him were powerfully built, determined.

"It's the town marshal!" Jud Crothers cried from the top of his cask.

"Stand back!" The official waved his pistol menacingly, then pointed to Jud Crothers. "Arrest that man!" he went on, addressing his deputies.

"What for?" Jud asked, removing the remains of a snowball from his coat collar.

"Sedition against the government!" the marshal growled, staring at Jud's hand-painted sign. "Go ahead, boys!" he nodded to the men with him.

One of them dragged Jud to the ground. The other, leaping to the top of the cask, tore down the sign.

Tom, furious, turned on the marshal.

"This is an outrage!" he cried. "The man has done nothing, said nothing, against the government. He came here to welcome a member of Congress. . . ."

"Hold your tongue, young fellow!" the marshal snapped, "or I'll arrest you as well!"

Tom's companions drew closer about him, muttering. Strong, sturdy country boys, patriotic to the core, they were in no mood to be threatened, dragooned by a petty government official. Black looks met the marshal's frowning gaze.

"We're free men!" one of them muttered.

The marshal raised his pistol, pointing it toward the threatening crowd.

"Clear out . . . all of you!" he said, his cheeks purple with anger. "You're resisting an officer of the government. Clear out, or I'll fire!"

The young men did not move. Mr. Lyon rose in the sleigh.

"You're not fit to be a government official," he said to the marshal. "Put your weapon away! Young men," he went on to Tom and the others, "when I was thrown into jail, at Ver-gennes, five hundred Green Mountain Boys came to get me out. You know what I told them. If the government treats you unjustly don't resist with violence. Seek redress at the polls! That's the American way . . . the democratic way! Elect Thomas Jefferson to the presidency, and I'll warrant you the Anti-Sedition Laws will be repealed within three months!"

A cheer came from the crowd. Jud Crothers laid his hand on Tom's shoulder; in spite of a split lip from one of the snow-balls, a rapidly closing eye, he did not seem at all depressed.

"Mr. Lyon's right, Tom," he said. "Drive my horse and sleigh home, will you? Explain things to my wife. Tell her I'm just another victim of Federalist tyranny. Don't worry; there aren't jails enough in the country to hold all the friends of free speech and never will be! Nobody can muzzle the press— or stop the voice of the people! It can't be done. Not ever! Hurrah for liberty! Hurrah for Tom Jefferson, our next presi-dent!" The fiery little man turned to the sleigh. "Good luck, Mr. Lyon. You tell those fellows down in Congress that Jud Crothers expects them to do their duty!" Grinning, he allowed the marshal to lead him up the street.

The next time that Tom saw the little farmer was at the door of his cell. Jud was still smiling, although his ruddy face had grown thinner and he seemed somewhat pale. For his offense he had been sentenced to pay a fine of four hundred dollars, and to spend one year in jail.

"What's the news, Tom?" he asked, thrusting a gnarled hand through the bars.

"Good news, Jud." Tom told him. "Mr. Jefferson is elected."

"Jumping Jehoshaphat! You don't mean it!"

"I certainly do. Just got the word from a man down at Vernon's Tavern. The electors tied, half for Mr. Jefferson, half for Aaron Burr. That threw the vote into the House of Representatives; they chose Mr. Jefferson on the thirty-sixth ballot."

"Glory be!" Jud exclaimed fervently.

"You'll soon be out," Tom added.

Jud Crothers stared at him, his shoe-button eyes snapping.

" 'Tain't gittin' out I'm thinkin' about, son," he said gravely . . . "It's what Tom Jefferson's election is going to mean to the country."

With pride I watched the citizens of the new American Republic vindicate the principles of democracy by settling their differences at the polls. At last a great nation had shown that its ideals could be maintained by an appeal to reason, rather than to force. With the election of Thomas Jefferson to the presidency of the United States, all that Washington and his ragged armies had fought for became realities. The people had proven their ability to rule, under the law.

Hopefully I turned my eyes toward the south, where a vast continent stirred restlessly under the galling yoke of foreign masters. Soon the subject peoples of that fruitful region, inspired by the example of their northern neighbors, began to demand a voice in the government of their affairs. Spanish rule, always cruel and oppressive, had become weakened by European wars, and patriotic men throughout South America raised the banners of freedom from the Gulf of Mexico to Cape Horn.

In the Argentine I saw a great leader rise. José de San Martin, bringing Liberty to that country, and to Chile. Far to the North, in Venezuela, Simon Bolivar began his brilliant and meteoric career. Through all the lands to the west the Great Liberator swept like a pillar of fire, scaling the peaks of the Andes to win incredible victories, carrying my blazing torch southward until he met José de San Martin at the borders of Peru.

On the bloody field of Ayacucho, in the year 1824, I saw

the forces of freedom win their final victory, with the Spanish Viceroy of Peru sitting huddled and beaten in a peasant's hut, and the flag of Spain hauled down for the last time on the continent of South America. The people had spoken; the Western Hemisphere no longer paid tribute to Kings; it was to march henceforth under the banner of democracy.

STEP OF CONQUERORS

HEARING a clatter of hoofbeats on the road, Luis Gonzales ran out to meet his father. The late afternoon sunshine was clear and brilliant, but a keen, swift breeze from the peaks of the Andes gave a chill to the air.

Señor Gonzales climbed rather stiffly from his horse, tossing the reins to one of the mule drivers in his pack-train. He was a stout, ruddy man, as much at home in the saddle as on foot, but now he was tired, having ridden for many days.

He clapped his tall son on the back and went into the house. Luis's mother came running to greet him, a silver cup of *chicha* in her hands. Francisco Gonzales kissed his wife affectionately, then drank the fiery liquor.

"A long journey," he said, sinking into a chair covered with cowhide. "But I got a good price for the silver." Señor Gonzales owned a small silver mine in the hills near Cerro de Pasco, and was accounted a man of means.

"And what did you see, in Guayaquil?" his wife asked, smiling. "Anything new and strange? They say the women there are very good-looking."

Francisco Gonzales twirled his fierce moustache.

"I saw no women, Isabella *mia*, to compare with you," he said gravely. "But I did see two of the greatest men in South America . . . perhaps in the whole world."

"And who were they?" Luis asked quickly.

"General José de San Martin, the hero of Argentina, of Chile, and Simon Bolivar, the famous Liberator!"

Luis's eyes sparkled. They were gray eyes, like his mother's. She had red-gold hair, unusual in Peru, and was proud of her Castilian ancestry.

"I've heard about General San Martin," Luis said, taking his father's empty cup. "He freed the people of Argentina, didn't he? And then marched over the mountains to help Chile win her independence?"

"That's right, Son." Señor Gonzales nodded. "A great leader and patriot."

"But," Luis went on, puzzled, "they say he's brought his army into Peru to help *us* throw out the Spaniards, too. Why should he go to see Simon Bolivar? To ask his aid?"

"That, Luis, is a mystery. I heard in Guayaquil that General San Martin offered to join forces with Bolivar against Spain, but nothing came of it. Neither, it seems, could ask the other to serve under him, each being so great and famous. In the end, people at Guayaquil said, San Martin decided to withdraw his forces and leave the field to his younger and more active rival. Perhaps that is best."

"I think it's very silly," Luis's mother said. "Two armies are better than one. Everybody knows how brilliant a leader General San Martin is. What has this Bolivar done?"

Señor Gonzales regarded his wife indulgently. Women, he thought, could not be expected to know much about war or politics.

"He has not only liberated his own country, Venezuela, after a long and bloody struggle, but New Granada and Quito as well. They say his passage of the Andes, over the Páramo de Pisba, was the most heroic feat ever undertaken by mortal man! Like a march through Hell itself! A frozen Hell! Now he has set all the country free as far south as our own borders. An immense territory. Colombia, they call it, with Simon Bolivar as its supreme ruler. A king, almost. But he prefers the title of Liberator."

"You saw him, while in Guayaquil?" Luis asked eagerly.

"Yes. When he escorted General San Martin to the dock. To take ship back to Callao. There was a great crowd. I pushed my way forward until I stood no further from the gangplank than the length of this room. San Martin was very grave and dignified. A handsome figure, with a high, noble forehead and the stern, erect bearing of a soldier."

"And Simon Bolivar?"

"I'm afraid, Luis, he would have disappointed you. A small, sallow man, with sunken cheeks, bushy whiskers and such tiny hands and feet you might have thought they belonged to a woman. Not at all like a hero—until you caught sight of his eyes. Black as night, and flashing. They say that when he is angry no one can withstand the fire in them."

"I'd like to see him myself," Luis murmured.

"You may soon have a chance. I was told in Guayaquil that he will shortly march southward into Peru, keeping to the foothills wherever the Spaniards hold the coast, and gathering new recruits. Who knows? He may pass through Cerro de Pasco."

"I hope he does," Luis said. "Has he a large army?"

"No. Not yet. Only some six or seven thousand men. He will need many more to face the Spanish. La Serna, the Viceroy, has fifteen thousand, at least. . . ."

"Then this Bolivar would have been wiser," Luis's mother said, "to have accepted General San Martin's help."

"Yes." Señor Gonzales gnawed his gray moustache. "So many thought in Guayaquil. But the Great Liberator is a dangerous antagonist. A brilliant soldier. Over and over, by some clever ruse, he has snatched victory from defeat. And one of his generals, Antonio Sucre, is said to be the equal of his master. Peru may yet be free."

"Are you going to fight, Francisco?" Señora Gonzales asked.

"Not I." Her husband lit a thin *cigarro*. "That is a task for younger men. Besides, should Simon Bolivar fail, the Spaniards, in revenge, will slaughter all who have supported him, along with their families. Women and children no less than men. So it was in Venezuela, in New Granada, when at first Bolivar's armies were beaten. The streets of the towns ran red!" Señor Gonzales gazed uneasily at his wife and son. "I must think of you as well. To be free is indeed a blessing, but to be alive is a necessity, if one would enjoy it. Come, Isabella." Señor Gonzales got up from his chair. "I must show you the presents I brought from Guayaquil."

Luis went out to the road. Coming along it he saw two of his friends, Juan Aguilar and his brother Teodar. They had been shooting in the hills, and had brought back a white goose and three partridges.

"Hola, Luis!" Juan Aguilar said. "You should have gone with us. Did your father get back?"

"Yes. With important news."

"What news?"

"Simon Bolivar with his army is at Guayaquil."

"The Great Liberator?" Both boys shouted at once.

"Yes! He is marching into Peru, to·help us drive out the Spaniards. Father says he will almost certainly come by way of Cerro de Pasco. Gathering recruits."

Juan Aguilar, who was nineteen, sighted along the barrel of his fowling piece.

"Lucky I'm a good shot," he said.

"Why?" Luis asked him.

"Because I mean to join Simon Bolivar's army."

"I was thinking of doing the same thing," Luis said.

"So shall I," chimed in Teodar, who was the youngest of the three.

"Let us swear it," Juan said, putting out his hand. "As patriots it is our sacred duty to fight for our country."

Solemnly the three boys shook hands.

"Who goes back on his promise is a coward," Juan added. "We'll see you again, Luis, after supper."

Luis went back to the house. He did not say anything to his father about his plan to enlist.

Winter had come before the army of the Liberator reached Cerro de Pasco. Their tents whitened the hillsides about the small mining town. Each day the new regiments marched, training raw recruits. Francisco Gonzales complained that he was losing many of his best workmen from the mine.

Coming home early one evening he paused with a frown at Luis's bedroom door. It stood ajar and through the aperture he saw that which disturbed him.

"For what reason, my son," he asked sternly, stepping into the room, "are you packing your shoulder sack?"

Luis set the cowhide bag on the floor.

"I am going to join the Army of Liberation," he said gravely.

Señor Gonzales's frown grew darker; his moustache quivered with anger.

"I forbid it!" he exclaimed.

"But . . . why, sir?"

"You are too young."

Señor Gonzales' frown grew darker. "I forbid it!"

"Not too young to carry a musket, Father . . . and pull the trigger of it. Both the Aguilar boys are going. Teodar is only seventeen."

"That is Señor Aguilar's business, not mine. Or yours. You should think of your mother. Were anything to happen to you she would be heartbroken."

"If all mothers felt that way," Luis objected hotly, "how could Peru, or any other land, become free?"

"Also," the older man went on, "you are my only son. Who else will there be to run the mine, when my strength fails me? I command you to give up this mad idea."

Luis stood very straight. He was taller than his father by two inches at least, and his eyes, usually smiling, like his mother's, suddenly resembled gray ice.

"I have tried, sir, to obey you in all things, up to this moment," he said. "Now I cannot. My word is given. I must keep it, by morning, or be held a coward."

Señor Gonzales took a step backward. His face flushed a mottled red.

"Since you defy me, I must compel you!" he exclaimed. With a swift movement he drew the large iron key from the keyhole and backing into the hallway locked the heavy oak door from outside. His actions were so quick that by the time Luis reached the stout panels he was too late; the steel bolt had clicked home.

"Food and water will be passed through the window," came to him, very faintly, from the hall.

The windows of the room—there were two—faced a small garden, a walled patio, in which on summer nights the family gathered to talk, sometimes to eat, when the weather was especially hot. Luis, angry and humiliated, stood for a long time gazing through the handsome, wrought-iron gratings. Between their lower edges and the stone sill was room enough to pass a small, flat dish, a pannikin, but Luis' thoughts were not concerned with food. He was wondering, not pleasantly, what the two Aguilar boys would think, and say, when he failed to meet them at the Liberator's camp the following morning. "Coward," he muttered to himself. "A breaker of promises, oaths, a traitor to the cause of liberty, to Peru!" Black thoughts. Blame for something beyond his control would be bitter indeed.

The moon had risen, when Manuelo, one of the servants, crept to the window and pushed a plate of *frijoles* and a dish of water over the sill. The Indian boy came and went silently, saying nothing; Luis felt sure that his father had given him orders not to speak. Francisco Gonzales, when crossed, could be a martinet.

Luis ate his supper, then sat by the window for hours, watching the moonlight silver the flagstones and make a dark pattern of the window gratings on the floor. At last, feeling sleepy, he threw himself, fully dressed, on the bed. The garden remained deserted; there was no possible way in which he could escape, unless someone were to unlock his bedroom door.

Presently he fell asleep, and sleeping, dreamed. An angel, he thought, had entered the room, was standing beside his bed, was touching his lips with a slender forefinger. He opened his eyes, to see with astonishment the dim figure of his mother. He would have cried out had not her finger against his lips stopped him.

She spoke in a clear, small voice, scarcely more than a whisper. Her head was held high; her flower-like face against the moonlight was as white as the peaks of the Andes.

"Luis," she said, "your father has told me what he did and what you planned to do. He commanded me not to see you. For the first time since our marriage I must go against his wishes. I am a proud woman, my son. Proud of the honor of my family, of your honor. My people came from Spain, from old Castile. Their name has been respected for many generations as that of brave soldiers, of honorable men. No son of mine shall be false to those traditions, nor be named a coward by his fellows." Señora Gonzales paused, her eyes glowing.

"Then you . . . you will let me go?" Luis asked, sitting up in the bed.

"You must go! How could you live, in this our land of Peru, enjoying a freedom you had done nothing to gain or to uphold? Take your sack and leave before your father, waking, seeks to stop you. Fight bravely for the right! I shall pray for your safe return."

Luis sprang from the bed and kissed his mother joyfully. Her lips against his, her cheeks, were as cold as marble, but there were no tears in her eyes. There would be time enough, later, for weeping.

"Go you with God!" she whispered.

Luis picked up his sack, crept out through the garden, since by that way he need not pass his father's door. Dawn was approaching; he hurried to the crossroads where he and the Aguilar boys were to meet.

They came presently, their young faces grave.

"We knew you would not fail," Juan said. "I have spoken to the recruiting officer. His name is Morales. We are to meet him at the large tent just outside the entrance to the camp."

Captain Morales, a grizzled veteran of the wars in Venezuela, greeted them with a satisfied smile, writing their names in his book.

"Pedro!" he said to an orderly. "Here are three stout patriots. See that they are provided with uniforms. Then turn them out for drill. *Adiós,* young gentlemen. Fight well, for Simon Bolivar and for Peru."

Within an hour the three boys were marching and wheeling on the level field beside the camp, learning what duties a soldier must perform. It was hard, unceasing work, but they faced it bravely for the sake of a just and honorable cause. Each day Luis wondered if he would soon see Simon Bolivar, but the drillmaster told him that the Liberator was still at Guayaquil.

Then one clear bright morning word spread through the camp that Bolivar had arrived, and with General Sucre and other officers of his staff would inspect the newly organized army in a grand review. Swelled by recruits its numbers had well-nigh doubled during the past two months.

Simon Bolivar, proudly sitting a tall gray horse, seemed to Luis a noble figure as with flashing eyes he watched regiment after regiment march by. They greeted him with cheers, these youthful patriots, crying *"Viva el Libertador!"* and raising their arms in salute.

Later, a proclamation, prepared by the Commander-in-Chief himself was read to the troops.

"Soldiers!" it said. "You are about to complete the greatest task ever entrusted by Heaven to man—that of freeing a world from slavery!

"Soldiers! The foes whom you are about to vanquish boast of fourteen years of triumph. That means you are going to meet men worthy of pitting their arms against yours, which have flashed in a thousand battles!

"Soldiers! Peru and all America expect you to bring them Peace, the daughter of Victory! Even Liberal Europe gazes upon you, entranced, because the Liberty of the New World is the hope of the whole world! Will you deny that hope? No! No! You are invincible!"

Luis, listening to the Great Liberator's inspiring words, cheered lustily, along with the rest of his regiment. It was made up partly of seasoned veterans, partly of new recruits, and formed a section of the vanguard under command of General Cordova. This dashing young officer, from New Granada, was very popular; he had distinguished himself in previous battles by his gay and reckless courage and both Luis and Teodar Aguilar felt it an honor to serve under him. Juan Aguilar, because of his expert horsemanship, had been given a post as dispatch rider on General Sucre's headquarters staff, and Luis and Teodar saw little of him.

Immediately after the grand review the army at Cerro de Pasco broke camp to go in search of the enemy. They came up with one of the Viceroy's officers, General Canterac, at the Plain of Junin, near the shores of Lake Reyes, and there in the high mountain passes a fierce cavalry engagement was fought. Luis saw nothing of the battle; the foot soldiers, plodding wearily through the hills, arrived too late to be of service, and Simon Bolivar, in a rage, was forced to watch the Spanish withdraw in good order, although not until after they had sustained considerable losses.

Luis and the younger of the two Aguilar brothers, marching long hours each day, living on parched corn and beans, with only a scrap of meat occasionally, sleeping on the ground in all weathers, did not find the life of a soldier very thrilling. The veterans who had accompanied Simon Bolivar from Venezuela, however, laughed, saying they would find plenty of excitement before the campaign was over.

One night Juan Aguilar came galloping into camp with dispatches for General Cordova. He hunted up Luis and his brother while waiting for his horse to be watered and fed.

"Bad news," he said. "The Liberator has been forced to surrender the supreme command."

"What?" Luis stared at him in surprise. "You're joking, Juan."

"I tell you it's true."

"Why?"

Juan slapped his high boots with a riding whip.

"The Colombian Congress is dissatisfied at hearing of no victories. They've ordered him to resign his civil and military authority. Fools! What do they know, off there in Venezuela, about what is going on in Peru? Just when he's on the point of victory, too. I heard him storming at General Sucre when I was summoned to his tent. At first he was going to defy the order. Later, he said that as President of the Colombian Republic he must obey the Congress like any other ordinary citizen."

"I suppose," Luis muttered, "that proves him to be a great man."

"I suppose it does. He's gone to Lima, leaving General Sucre in chief command. I hear there's likely to be some fighting shortly. Our scouts report General Canterac at Matara. It must have been a bitter blow to the Liberator; he'd set his heart on winning this campaign." An orderly came up with Juan's horse. "Well, I must leave you. Good luck." Mounting, he galloped off.

When the news brought to General Cordova reached the men, there was bitter dissatisfaction; they followed their officers bravely at all times, but Simon Bolivar was their inspiration, their god. Thus the battle at Matara went indifferently, and the Viceroy's advance guard was able to retire in good order and join the main Spanish army at Ayacucho.

General Sucre, realizing that the supreme test had come, arranged his men for battle. Losses had reduced the patriot army to a scant seven thousand; the Viceroy's forces numbered over ten. To inspire his troops, lift the gloom in which Simon Bolivar's departure had thrown them, General Sucre rode out along the battle lines.

The Spanish were camped on the heights of Cundurcanca. On the plain facing them the patriot army stood, in three divi- sion, General Cordova commanding the vanguard on the right, General La Mar, who had been trained in the armies of Spain, at the center, and General Lara, veteran of Simon Bolivar's earlier campaigns, on the left. In the patriot ranks were not only soldiers of Venezuela, New Granada, Quito, Peru, but English, Scotch and Irish adventurers, lionhearted fighters who had followed Bolivar over the high Andes and braved death on a hundred fields to serve the cause of human liberty.

Facing his men General Sucre addressed them, making the one appeal he felt sure would reach their hearts.

"Remember your triumphs, your glories, your honor, your country!" he shouted. "And above all remember, and be worthy of, your great leader, Simon Bolivar!"

That was the spark needed to set their hearts aflame. Simon Bolivar! A roar of cheers went up for their absent chieftain.

"Viva!" the soldiers roared in one great voice. "Viva el Libertador!" So loud were their shouts that Simon Bolivar might almost have heard them in far-off Lima. Young General Cordova leaped from the saddle, his hair streaming, and in a frenzy of excitement drew a pistol and shot his horse dead.

"Should we be defeated, men," he cried, "you will know that I cannot ride off and leave you! *Viva Peru!*" The Spanish gunners on the heights of Cundurcanca, hearing the noise, thought that the patriots were advancing and at once began a furious cannonade.

Luis was not able, afterwards, to tell much concerning the details of that historic struggle. Many of them he never even saw, for smoke and dust swept like a pall over the wide field. From their position on the hills a column of Spanish infantry swept down in massed formation, bayonets fixed, aiming a furious attack at the center of the patriot lines. General Cordova, striding up and down before his men, impatiently awaited orders for a counterattack. The flank of the advancing column lay open; if he could strike them there. . . .

Luis Gonzales, being a new recruit, stood at the end of one of the rear ranks. Hearing hoofbeats, he turned his head. Through clouds of smoke a horseman was riding toward him, a hundred or more yards away. Had the enemy launched a cavalry attack, he wondered, designed to take the patriot army in flank and rear? As a puff of wind lifted the smoke momentarily Luis gave a cry. There was but one rider, on a big sorrel horse with a great white blaze on its forehead! Juan Aguilar's horse! Luis had seen the animal too often, at home, not to recognize him now. As the pall of battle once more descended, a roll of musket fire came from the advancing Spanish column and horse and rider crashed to the ground.

In that moment all the rules of discipline which had been drilled into Luis's mind for the past three months vanished. His friend was there, in danger! Wounded, perhaps! Shot down! Leaping from the ranks he raced at top speed across the field. Shouts followed him as he plunged through clouds of dust and smoke but he did not turn; his only thought was to go to Juan's aid.

Juan Aguilar, his face white with pain, lay with one leg pinned beneath the dead body of his horse. The big sorrel had been shot through the heart. Before Luis could speak Juan opened his eyes and held out a shaking hand. There was a bit of paper crushed between his dust-stained fingers.

"For General Cordova!" he cried in an agonized voice. "An order from the Commander in Chief! To charge . . . !"

"But . . . Juan! You . . . you are hurt. . . ."

Juan Aguilar made no reply; he had fainted.

Luis knew what he had to do. No time to aid his friend, to try to rescue him from the crushing weight of his horse. Even now the fate of the battle might hang by a thread. He tore the dispatch from Juan's nerveless fingers, ran panting back to the patriot lines. General Cordova, striding up and down like a caged animal before his impatient men, paused amid a volley of curses. Luis thrust the folded paper into his hand.

"From General Sucre!" he gasped, breathless. "An order . . . charge!"

The young commander of the vanguard did not stop to read the order. Raising his sword he addressed the surging ranks that faced him.

"Arms . . . as you please!" he shouted. "Step". . . . For an instant his lips curved in a gay, proud smile. . . . "Step . . . of conquerors! Forward!" In the next moment two thousand desperate men hurled themselves like an avalanche against the flank of the advancing Spanish column, now so close that the flash of their bayonets could be seen.

Not even Spanish discipline, Spanish courage, could check the fury of that charge. Here were men advancing indeed with the step of conquerors, to beat down the forces of oppression and win victory for the Great Liberator, for Simon Bolivar and Peru.

Luis, swept along in that breath-taking assault, knew nothing of what was taking place on other parts of the battlefront. Only later did he learn of the gallant work of the patriot cavalry under their English leader, General Miller; of the fierce attacks by the Vargas Battalion, the Hussars, supporting General La Mar at the center; of the reserves, sent in by General Sucre at the critical moment to crush the Spanish right. Through the smoke and dust of battle the vanguard of young General Cordova swept on, fighting with the fury of demons behind their gay and fearless leader, hurling the veteran troops of Spain aside, driving on and on, up the slopes of Cundurcanca, over the Spanish batteries stationed there until, conquerors all, they reached even the headquarters of the Viceroy

La Serna himself, surrounded him and his staff with a ring of steel!

Luis, flushed and breathless, watched La Serna, bleeding from a wound in the head, give up his sword. All around men were cheering, shouting, waving their caps. It was a tremen- dous moment, yet throughout that fierce charge one picture kept flashing before Luis Gonzales's eyes—a picture of Juan Aguilar, lying crushed and senseless beneath his fallen horse. He turned to Teodar, grasping his arm.

"Come!" he said, pointing down the hill. "Your brother. . . ."

"But . . . we should ask permission. . . .' '

"No time, now . . . nor any need. The battle's won! Hurry! He may be desperately hurt! Even dying. . . ."

Through groups of wildly cheering men the two boys ran, down the long slope, across the battle-torn field at the foot of it, toward the point where Juan had been left at the beginning of the charge.

The sorrel horse was there, but not its rider. Now that the battle was over, some peasants had come to give aid to the wounded; from one of them Luis learned that Juan was at a nearby cottage with no worse injury than a broken leg.

They found him, lying on a heap of straw, conscious, but suffering great pain.

"Luis!" he muttered faintly. "Did you deliver that order . . . to General Cordova?"

"Yes. Just in time. The Spanish are beaten. Didn't they tell you?"

"One of the men who carried me here said so. I could not believe. . . ."

"It is true. We've won a great victory. I myself saw the Viceroy give up his sword!"

Juan Aguilar raised a trembling hand.

"Viva el Libertador!" he cried feebly. *"Viva Peru!"*

"As soon as your leg is well again," Luis said, "we can go home. Now I must find you a doctor."

A month later the three arrived in Cerro de Pasco, marching, in spite of Juan's newly healed leg, with the step of conquerors. Señor Gonzales, filled with pride in spite of his former objections, gave a great feast in Luis's honor . . . which is the way of fathers. Señora Gonzales lit six candles and wept on her tall son's shoulder . . . which is the way of mothers.

Simon Bolivar, offered a crown by wildly cheering multitudes, refused it, saying he preferred to be known simply as The Liberator . . . which was the way of a truly great man.

On the field of Ayacucho the power of Spain in the Western Hemisphere was finally broken. The forces of liberty had freed a whole continent from foreign rule.

I held my torch high as I saw the South American nations, one by one, take their places among the free republics of the Western World. Yet I knew that in the North the fight for true democracy was still not finally won.

Thomas Jefferson had proclaimed the immortal principle that all men are created equal. It remained for another great democratic leader to declare that no nation founded on Jefferson's humanitarian doctrine could endure part slave and part free.

Reason should have shown men the truth of that declaration, but four years of bitter and unhappy warfare were needed before the words of both Jefferson and Abraham Lincoln were vindicated, and the two halves of the great American Republic became finally joined in one firm and indissoluble Union.

Happily I looked on as peace and prosperity came to bless the people of America. Now at last it seemed that free men, following the ways of truth and justice I had so often pointed out, were to scale new heights on the road of human progress, multiplying civilized comforts, conquering poverty and disease, overcoming distance by land, sea and air, daring and achieving as no nation had ever dared and achieved before. A nation devoted to the arts of peace, with malice toward none, with charity for all.

But across the sea I watched with anxiety a strong and restless people, dreaming of conquest, demanding for themselves a larger place in the sun. A militant people, whose youth had been taught that on them lay the task of bringing a new and superior culture to the world; a people contemptuous of the peaceful ways of democracy, holding that might, not right, should rule the affairs of men. Their arrogant demands brought about a great and devastating conflict, in which a large part of Europe became involved.

Year after year I watched the people of America grow increasingly indignant as ruthless methods of warfare, the sinking of merchant vessels, the destruction by secret agents of their home industries, the German boasts of world domination, all challenged their democratic ideals. Convinced at last that those ideals were in danger, the great western Republic threw its whole weight into the struggle. Soon I saw millions of peace-loving Americans fighting on foreign battlefields in a war they hoped might forever end war, and so bring the principles of reason and justice, of government by the people for the people, to a confused and unhappy world. Men of good will everywhere prayed that through democracy the voice of the toiling millions of Europe might be heard, demanding a peace in which the burden of armaments would be lifted from their backs, disputes between nations settled around a council table, and age-old hates forgotten, in the effort to build a new and better civilization for all mankind.

For these things the American people fought. With no thought of material reward they gave their lives to defend, to uphold, abroad, the ideals of liberty, of equality, of democracy which had brought them such splendid progress, such fruitful rewards at home. No nation ever went to war in a nobler or more unselfish cause. I watched the conflict anxiously, hoping that at last the light of my torch would be seen by all men, to guide their footsteps in the ways of justice, of truth.

ARMISTICE

DAVE EVANS, dressing for the Armistice Day parade, found that his uniform was becoming too tight for him. He had gained considerable weight since the never-to-be-forgotten morning when he'd gone aboard the transport, a youngster of nineteen, bound for France. That had been ten years ago. The boys were singing "Over There," he remembered, ready for any sacrifice to make the world safe for democracy. It was pleasant, he thought, giving another tug at his belt, to know they had succeeded. Poland, Czechoslovakia, Finland, a dozen other countries, including Germany itself, now had democratic governments and were doing well. Even China was about to become a republic. Peace pacts were being signed right and left; the League of Nations had outlawed war. He was glad he'd done his bit to help along the good work, in spite of a few grumblers

234

who thought America should have kept out of the fight. There were always people like that, always had been, even in Washington's time and Lincoln's. People without ideals. . . .

He turned as his wife came to the door.

"Here's Uncle Jesse Slocum," she said. "You're going to drive him in town for the parade."

"Right! Hello, Uncle Jesse! You got here early. Come in and rest your dogs. How're you feeling? Able to march with the boys?"

The silver-haired old veteran nodded. His faded blue uniform was too big for him and like his face showed many wrinkles, but there was still fire in his bright blue eyes.

"Purty fair, son," he said, sinking into a chair. "Purty fair for an old fellow. Not so spry as I used to be, though. I can remember, at Chickamauga, marchin' all night to come up with the Johnny Rebs—and goin' into battle next day fresh as a daisy, without a bite of breakfast except some hardtack."

Dave smiled at the old soldier; he had heard the story of Chickamauga many times before.

"I've just been thinking, Uncle Jesse," he said, "how some folks are beginning to say we boys shouldn't have gone over to France, ten years ago. I suppose they said the same thing when you went to war."

"They did indeed, son. You never heard anything like the abuse heaped on poor Mr. Lincoln. I was at Gettysburg when he made his famous address." The old veteran's eyes took on a warmer glow. "That was a day for you! Flags wavin', bands playin', soldiers everywhere. First time I'd ever seen the President. A tall, bent man, with a tired, sad face. I was right close to the reviewing stand. Remember thinkin' he had powerful big feet."

"But his speech," Dave exclaimed. "Weren't you thrilled by that? About government of the people, by the people, for the people, not perishing from the earth? Why . . . they teach it to kids in school."

"I know, son." Uncle Jesse nodded. "But nobody paid much attention to what he said, at the time. Wasn't 'till later on folks came to understand we hadn't been fightin' just to free a passel of slaves, but to preserve democracy . . . preserve the Union." For a time he watched Dave lacing his shoes, then went on in a thin, dry voice. "It was worth it, son. All that fightin'. Even dyin'. As Mr. Lincoln said that day, those men at Gettysburg did not die in vain, although a good many people thought different, at the time. Same with you boys, in France. Now they cheer us both in parades. Folks are funny thataway . . . some folks."

Dave stood up, put on his tunic.

"I'm dead against war, as a general proposition," he said. "So are most of us boys who went overseas. It's a dirty, lousy business. Crawling like rats through muddy trenches. Sleeping in filthy dugouts. Seeing men die by inches hanging on barbed wire right in front of your eyes, without being able to help them. War's hell, all right. I'm for peace every time. That's what we went over there to fight for . . . peace. Now we've got it. And you can bet your life, Uncle Jesse, that the fellows who stayed at home and are enjoyin' the peace we gave them will do most of the cheering and shouting. Hand me that tin lid, will you?"

The silver-haired veteran took Dave's steel helmet from the table, held it for a moment between his white fragile fingers.

"We didn't have any such contraptions to purtect our heads in *my* day," he said, touching the surface of the metal. "Reckon without it the bullet that made this dent would have finished you." He indicated a small depression in the steel.

"Wasn't a bullet," Dave laughed.

"Bayonet, maybe," Uncle Jesse went on. "Or shell splinter."

"No." Dave glanced at his watch; he was still laughing. "I'd clean forgot about that dent, Uncle Jesse. Funny . . . got it on Armistice Day, ten years ago. There's plenty of time, before we need start, if you'd like to hear the story."

"Sure would, son." The old gentleman sank comfortably back in his chair. "Never heard you talk much about your doings in France. Modest, aren't you?"

Dave Evans cocked the steel helmet jauntily over one ear, glanced at himself in the mirror.

"Some hero," he said, grinning. "As I've told you, Uncle Jesse, I got that dent in my lid on Armistice Day, in 1918. The real one, I mean; we'd had a false alarm, just the week before. Never found out who started that story, but some of our boys, thinking it was true, climbed out of the trenches to say hello to the Heines facing us. They came back in a hurry, believe me, when Fritz opened up with machine guns. So after that we didn't pay much attention to armistice rumors. Figured they were just German tricks.

"The night before the real one came off, I was sent with a message to regimental headquarters. We were up in the Argonne, holding an advanced post, with our communications smashed by artillery fire and the outfit cut off. A couple of runners had already been sent out to try and establish contact, but I guess they ran into trouble, for the ammunition we were so badly in need of didn't show up. So along about midnight I was elected to make another attempt. Guess our Captain had heard I'd been a Boy Scout, or something.

"I hadn't so far to travel, but the night was pretty dark, and it's tough going at any time in that Argonne country. I plugged along, watching my step, moving careful and slow so as not to lose my way and bump into one of the enemy outposts. They had machine gun nests all through the forest, up in trees and other places you'd never think of. Well, to cut a long story short, I made it all right, and half an hour later was on my way back with a message from the officer in command.

"The darkness was so thick by this time I practically had to feel my way. It was around 2 A.M., with heavy mist in the woods, and I was afraid every minute I'd take the wrong path and end up in the enemy's lines. Tricky place, the Argonne Forest, especially at night. I didn't want to get lost in it.

"As a matter of fact, that's just what I did, although I wasn't sure until I stepped through a fringe of bushes into what looked

like a plowed field. I hadn't seen any plowed fields on my outward trip, so I knew right off I'd missed my way somehow and
got on the wrong track.

"There was more light, in that open space, than back under
the trees, and halfway across it I could make out what looked
like a small farmhouse, with a stable yard and some outbuild-
ings beyond. The windows of the place didn't show any lights,
but of course you wouldn't expect any at that time of night.
If there were people living in the house, they'd have been in
bed, asleep.

"I started across the field, thinking maybe I might find somebody who would direct me back to our lines, even if I had to
wake them up. I hadn't the least idea where I was, or which
way to turn, and the prospect of wandering about in the woods
all night wasn't inviting.

"I moved cautiously, not taking any chances. For all I knew,
there might be an enemy listening post in the house. When I'd
got about a dozen yards from it, I thought I saw somebody
moving in the stable yard, behind a low wall. I dropped flat
on my face, lay there, expecting every minute to hear the crack
of a rifle, the hum of a bullet coming my way. Or maybe a
flare, to show me stretched out on the ground. But nothing
happened.

"Naturally I couldn't be sure it was an enemy I'd seen. But
on the other hand there seemed no good reason why any member of a farmer's family should be dodging about the barnyard
at three o'clock in the morning. Then, from the other side of

the wall, I heard something that gave me a laugh. The faint mooing of a cow.

"That made me feel entirely different. The way I figured it, if there was a cow, there must be people living in the house. And the Germans hadn't been around or they'd have carried off the cow, same as they did all farm animals. So I got up, holding my rifle ready in case I'd made a mistake, and went along the wall until I came to the door of the house.

"My first idea was to rap on it, try to wake somebody up. Then I noticed the door was standing slightly ajar, as if who-ever had last gone in or out hadn't closed it properly. With the muzzle of my rifle I pushed the door open.

"Ahead of me stretched what I figured was the main hall of the house, pitch black, and quiet as a grave. I listened for a moment, thinking I might hear someone snore, or turn over in bed, maybe, but there was nothing stirring. The place gave me the creeps, it was so still."

"Pretty soon my eyes got used to the darkness and I made out a lighter space on my left, figured it must be an open door-way leading into a room. I tiptoed inside, looked around. It *was* a room, not quite so dark, because there were three long French windows in it, two at the side, and a third at the far end, facing the stable-yard. The window at the end was open; I could feel a faint breeze blowing through. Enough light came in to make objects about me visible, but only as vague shadows.

"I stood still for a couple of minutes, trying to get my bear-ings. Between me and the end window I saw a long, flat object

I thought must be a bed. Whether there was anybody in it or not I couldn't tell. Figuring I might as well find out, I stepped forward, walking on my toes. Just as I got to the side of the bed, one of the boards in the floor gave a loud creak.

"I stopped as if I'd been shot. But it wasn't the sound of the creaky floor board that stopped me. I'd seen something. At the open window leading to the yard. A dark figure was standing in it, outlined against the blue night sky. A man—a soldier— I could tell that from his helmet. A German helmet—I knew the shape. He had one arm raised, thrown back, and was grip- ping something in his fingers that I didn't need two guesses to tell me was a hand grenade. I felt sure he couldn't see me standing there in the dark, but he'd heard that floor board creak and was all set to let fly with his potato masher if it creaked again.

"I had a finger on the trigger of my rifle, knew I couldn't miss him at that distance, firing from the hip. It wasn't over ten feet. But I also knew if he pitched forward, as he was bound to do, that grenade would come crashing into the room along with him and blow me to little bits. So I didn't shoot. . . ."

"Jumpin' Jerusalem!" Uncle Jesse Slocum muttered, sitting bolt upright in his chair. "What happened then? What *did* you do?"

"Nothing," Dave Evans said. "Just stood there with my fin- ger on the trigger waiting for Fritz to make the first move. Instead, he barked out something in German that I knew meant, 'Who's there?'

"Naturally I didn't answer him. I figured the minute he heard an American voice he'd let go with the grenade. So I decided that unless I wanted to be killed right off, the best thing I could do was to shoot first and then drop on the floor, hoping the grenade would go sailing over my head. I'd just started to press the trigger—all this had taken only a second or two—when I heard a voice from the bed! A child's voice! Terribly frightened! Calling out one word in the dark . . . *Maman!*"

"Gosh A'mighty!" Uncle Jesse said. "A child!"

"Yep. Just a scared kid, waked up by that German soldier's voice, crying for its mother. You could of knocked me over with a feather I was so startled. But I didn't say anything, or move. The Heine didn't either, except to lower his hand grenade, which made me feel a lot better, as I still had him covered with my gun.

"Right off there came a noise from the bed, like slats creaking, and all of a sudden a small spark blazed up. The kid had scratched a match—was lighting a candle on the bedside table at her elbow.

"You know how a candle begins to burn. Just a thin blue flame at first. But it was enough to show a girl about ten years old sitting up in the bed, her eyes so big and frightened they seemed to fill her whole face. I thought she looked not only scared, but sick.

"A minute later the wax of the candle had melted and it began to give off a good bright light—plenty for that German

"Drop that potato masher, Fritz!"

soldier to see me—see it wouldn't be healthy to start anything, with my rifle pointed straight at his chest. My fingers were doing exercises on the trigger, but I couldn't have pulled it, not with that kid sitting between us—any more, I guess, than he could have thrown his hand grenade. We both stood there staring at each other like a couple of cigar-store Indians, while the youngster in the bed kept crying for her mother.

"Pretty soon the situation got on my nerves.

" 'Put down your potato masher, Fritz,' I said, hoping he'd understand me. 'I'm not going to shoot. Way things are I guess we'll have to declare an armistice—a little private one of our own.'

"As I say, I was afraid he wouldn't understand what I was driving at, but he did. This Heine—he was a nice looking young fellow about my own age—began to grin. He'd learned English at school, he told me afterwards, understood what I'd said at once. I told him to put all his junk—he had a rifle in his left hand—on a sofa at one side of the room, which he did, watching me closely. Then I lowered my gun, parked it there too. Naturally I'd kept him covered, but he didn't try any monkey business, and pretty soon we'd both got rid of our hardware and were shaking hands across the bed.

" 'A treaty of peace, Kamerad,' he said, 'while we see what for the *Maedchen* can be done, yes?'

" 'That's the idea,' I told him. 'Looks to me as if the young-ster's kind of sick.' She was sitting there, her eyes like saucers, still scared but not so much after she saw us put down our guns. I leaned over, tried to take her wrist, to feel her pulse, but she drew away from me, staring.

"The Heine, who could speak French as well, talked to the kid for a few minutes, softly, got her quieted down, asked her some questions. Then he turned to me and explained, in his copybook English, that the youngster had been taken sick earlier in the evening and her mother had gone somewhere to fetch a doctor. Her father was in the army, she said.

" 'The child is with fever suffering,' he went on, 'and wishes water to drink. We should some for her find, isn't it?'

" 'Right, buddy,' I said. 'You stay here and keep her company while I scout around and see if I can't locate a well.' So I went out to the yard, unarmed, wondering if I wasn't an awful sap and wouldn't find a gun poked in my ribs when I got back. But this Heine and I had shaken hands, declared an armistice, and I sort of felt he'd stick by his word.

"After a while I found a pump, but the drinking cup was chained to it so I carried the water back in my tin hat. Fritz was sitting on the edge of the bed feeding the youngster bits of milk chocolate. She seemed very glad to get the water and drank about a pint. The room was feeling pretty cold by this time—it was close to the middle of November, you know—but I found some sticks of wood in a box beside the hearth, and soon had a good blaze going in the chimney place.

"The kid got sleepy, then, what with the warmth and her fever, so this Heine and I—his name was Ernst, he told me, Ernst Gauss—sat in front of the fire and talked.

"Seems he'd been at school during the early part of the war, and had only just been called to the front. His people lived in Leipsic, he said, and he had a kid sister about the age of the little girl in the bed. As for the war, he thought it was a crime the way the German people were being encircled and starved by the brutal English and French and couldn't understand why we Americans had taken their part.

"I told him that the English and French weren't any more brutal than other folks, far as I could see, and the reason we'd come into the war was to make the world safe for democracy. We believed in freedom, I said, and wouldn't stand for the Kaiser sinking our ships on the high seas, or blowing up our ammunition factories at home, and anyway, Americans hadn't any use for Emperors with shining swords who wanted to conquer the world. It didn't sound so very convincing, the way I explained things, but politics never were my strong point.

"Then this kid started in with a long song and dance about Germany being selected by providence to bring what he called *Kultur* to the world, and how she wanted a place in the sun, and that didn't make much sense either. In the end we both agreed that if ordinary, everyday people could get together and talk things over, maybe there wouldn't be any wars, and I said that was what we all hoped in America, after this one was over.

"We gave up politics, then, and began to talk about ourselves, which was better. Ernst admitted that what he really wanted to do was study medicine and become a famous doctor.

And I said my ambition was to go into the garage business and maybe some day get married to a girl I knew back home. When he had tried to tell me about the Kaiser and all, it sounded just like a piece he'd learned out of a book, but as soon as we got to talking about our personal affairs, our home folks, I found he was a regular guy, just like anybody else. I figured all that other stuff was just bunk he'd been filled up with, propaganda, to make him want to fight. Maybe he thought the same thing about me; I don't know. We sat there chewing the rag until the sun came up and then we started to think about breakfast.

"The kid in the bed was still asleep so we sneaked out to the yard, where the pump was, and made a meal off our emergency rations. Didn't look through the house to see if there was any grub around for fear we might wake up the child. I asked Ernst if he knew how to milk a cow, but he said he didn't, and neither did I, so we gave up that idea. We both of us knew we ought to be getting back to our outfits; seems he'd got lost the night before, same as I did. There was some sniping going on, a couple of miles away, and farther along the lines both sides were putting over some heavy stuff, but all in all the front was fairly quiet.

"About eight o'clock we saw a man and woman coming toward the house and went to meet them, figuring it must be the child's mother, and the doc. Which it was. The woman looked pale and thin, and seemed scared to death at seeing us, until Ernst told her the kid was O. K. The doctor, a big gray man in a shabby frock coat, listened to what we had to say and

then he and the woman went into the house. Ernst and I sat
on the grass, waiting.

"Pretty soon the doctor came out again, said the youngster
was ill with typhoid fever, but he thought she'd come through
all right, given the proper food and care. I had a few francs
in my jeans and handed them to the old fellow, told Ernst to
explain the money was for medicines or anything else the kid
might need. Then Ernst gave him some money, too.

"The doctor mumbled his thanks, and said with a queer,
funny kind of a smile that we were a couple of fine boys and
he was glad to see we'd made friends, instead of shooting each
other full of holes, now that the war was over.

"Naturally I didn't understand his French until Ernst translated it for me and then we both wanted to know what he
meant by saying the war was over. The two of them jabbered
for a moment and then Ernst turned to me and shouted the
good news—that an armistice had been declared beginning at
five o'clock that morning, and the order to cease firing was set
for eleven!

" 'In less than two hours,' the doctor said, pulling out a big
silver watch, 'we shall, thank the good God, have peace!'

"Well, sir, I stood there staring at Ernst, flabbergasted. If
it hadn't been for that little French girl calling for her mother
in the middle of the night we'd both of us been dead as mack-
erels, without doing a bit of good to our countries!

"Then the woman came out of the house carrying a tray
with glasses of homemade wine on it and after thanking Ernst

and me for looking after her kid, offered us each a glass, to drink to the war being over.

"The doctor raised his, made a little speech, which Ernst translated to me.

" 'There need never have been any war,' he growled, 'but for vicious teachers, telling their young people senseless and stupid lies! Preaching doctrines of racial superiority, one over another—of envy and hate! There is only one Teacher to whom men should listen in such matters and He taught peace and love! If all would follow His doctrines, there would be no more wars in the world. But selfish and ambitious leaders, to further their own evil ends, continue to corrupt the minds and souls of their people, teaching even school children to march with gun and sword, glorifying brute force! Only when we have gotten rid of such creatures can the world be safe for decent men. France is a democratic, home-loving country. It has never harbored designs of conquest against its neighbors. It has wished only peace!' The gray-haired doctor turned to Ernst, standing beside him. 'You are a German,' he said sternly. 'I am a Frenchman, and therefore your enemy—at least for the next two hours. I condemn those who have taught you to hate me . . . to hate my people! The Armistice will not go into effect until eleven o'clock. If you consider it your duty to shoot me, as your soldiers have shot many innocent civilians throughout the country, do so. My duty as a doctor is to save life, not take it. *Vive la France!*' The old fellow stalked off, without bothering to so much as turn his head. Ernst glanced

at his rifle—we'd both brought our guns out of the house,
when we ate breakfast—but of course he hadn't any idea of
using it, and the doctor knew he hadn't. What hurt Ernst most
was that remark the old fellow made about saving life, not
taking it. Ernst wanted to be a doctor, too.

"Well, we sat there on the grass, waiting for the hour set
to cease firing. He and I, being soldiers, instead of a civilian
like the doctor, ought by rights to have pitched into each other
. . . until eleven o'clock. But of course we didn't—or go to
look for our outfits, either. Figured we'd like as not get shot
on the way. It made no sense, with the war as good as over,
so we stayed where we were.

"It seemed a long and tiresome wait but at last a clock inside
the house struck eleven and the firing up the line stopped cold.
All we could hear was somebody playing a bugle, far off. The
Marseillaise, it was.

"This German kid turned to me, began to jabber something
about our now being brothers. I let out a yell, took off my tin
lid, and threw it up in the air as far as I could. When the
darned thing came down it hit the sharp corner of a rock.
That's what made the dent. Can't even claim I got it in the
war—that had been over a good half-minute." Dave took off
the helmet, grinning at the small mark in the steel. "Some hero!"

"Did you ever hear anything more about the German boy?"
Uncle Jesse asked, putting on his own broad-brimmed hat.

"Sure. Got a letter from him last week. He usually writes,
along about Armistice day each year, reminding me how we

almost blew each other's blocks off, that night in the Argonne. He's studying medicine in Paris now. Thinks the French are a wonderful people. Thinks the war was a good thing, too, because it brought peace . . . lasting peace. I hope he's right."

"Amen!" Uncle Jesse said, straightening his thin shoulders.

"Time to start, Dave!" a woman's voice called up the stairs. "You don't want to be late for the parade."

Arm and arm, the two veterans marched toward the stair-case, chins high.

In the distance they could hear a band, playing "The Battle Hymn of the Republic."

At last the Great War came to an end, and I looked on hope-fully as the nations turned to peace. New and independent states, free at last to realize their ancient aspirations, began to prosper. Armaments were reduced, treaties of amity signed, and men everywhere took new heart, believing that a happier era had dawned for the world.

But the peace that had been gained at such cost in blood and treasure was a perilous one, beneath which lay hate and mount-ing fear. Countless millions, stripped of their possessions by war, longed not for freedom but for security, and sought it at the hands of unscrupulous demogogues, while the guardians of the peace looked on with fatuous smiles.

In Russia I saw revolution, begun by honest men, fall into the hands of cruel and bloodthirsty fanatics. Soon the Russian people, freed from the bitter rule of their Czars, promised a new Utopia, found themselves in the grip of a tyranny more hard and ruthless than the one they had overthrown. I watched their Red Dictator build his mighty army, knowing well that he too, like the many who had preceded him from Alexander to Napoleon, would before long follow the age-old pathway of the Conquerors.

In Italy as well I saw an unhappy and impoverished people turn for security to a vain and crafty leader, who dreamed of restoring the grandeur that was Rome, with himself another

Caesar. With sad heart I watched him sweep aside constitutional rule, destroy the liberties of a peace-loving and artistic
people, set up a military dictatorship. To satisfy his ambitions
I saw him send his legions, armed with bombs and poison gas,
to cheap victory over helpless African tribesmen. Boasting of
Empire, he had succeeded only in degrading Rome's ancient
Eagles to the level of vultures, preying on the dead.

In Germany, smoldering with resentment under the harsh
terms of the victors, I saw an even more sinister figure rise.
Her people, having neither the training to understand nor the
will to follow the ways of democracy, turned to an Austrian
megalomaniac who promised to avenge all their real and fancied
wrongs by force of arms. Shrewdly playing upon their vanity,
flattering them with fables of a master race, he preached a
monstrous doctrine of both religious and political hatred,
through which his followers were to gain dominion over the
earth. No law of God or man would be permitted to stop them;
their glorious task was to destroy democratic civilization, build
on its ruins a New Order in which they, a chosen few, would
be the masters, served by conquered peoples, waxing fat on the
wealth of a looted world.

Even in the Far East I saw the ramparts of democracy
crumbling. For years I had watched the people of China
struggle to throw off the meaningless bonds and ceremonies of
their classic past in favor of republican government. Ardent
and courageous young men and women, filled with ideals taught
them in the West, had labored patiently to build a great new

democracy. Now they were forced to defend their country against a strong and ruthless aggressor. Well might the people of China have lost heart as they saw their richest provinces captured, their cities burned, their women and children slaughtered by a rain of bombs. Instead they bravely fought on, moving armies, factories, even schools and universities westward, students and teachers alike tramping the roads, carrying books and equipment for thousands of miles to safer locations, that the lamps of knowledge, of learning might not be blackened out.

Over Europe the clouds of war grew ever darker, as the new Dictators prepared their armies for conquest, and the great democracies slept. But the men of China were not sleeping. I held my torch proudly over their scorched cities, their ravaged countrysides, knowing that here was a nation ready to die if need be rather than surrender its liberties; a people gallant and unafraid.

INDEPENDENCE DAY

MILE after mile the road wound westward, narrow and twisting and hard. Ching-li, pushing the heavily loaded wheelbarrow before him, wondered if the thin gray ribbon he had
followed for so many weeks would ever come to an end.

At times it climbed long rocky hillsides, treeless and bare.
At others it crept timidly through scorched and blackened villages, mere heaps of ashes and crumbling walls. Now and then
it came to streams, spanned by high-arching stone bridges, or
muddy rivers, only to be crossed in large flat boats. Sometimes
hours passed before the little caravan with its bullock wagons,
wheelbarrows, rickshaws and carts, its line of heavily bur-
dened porters, to say nothing of teachers and students, had
been safely transported to the farther side. Only a few of the
older members of the faculty, whose feet had given out, were

able to ride; the others trudged along with their classes, leaving the wagons and carts for more precious burdens—books,
instruments, and countless bits of equipment so necessary to a
modern seat of learning.

Ching's wheelbarrow held, among other things, a spectroscope, wrapped in an old cotton blanket, and fifty or more
technical books which Dr. Wu-sung, the professor of physics
and a Cornell graduate, had placed in his special care. Ching,
his eyes searching the sky, lived in constant fear that some of
the Japanese warplanes so frequently to be seen overhead might
suspect what rare burdens the carts and wagons and barrows
carried, and drop their deadly eggs. From the air, however,
the caravan appeared merely as another string of refugees, fleeing westward, and unworthy of a high-priced explosive bomb.

Ching had three books of his own in the wheelbarrow: a
Bible presented to him while at mission school, a history of the
United States, and a paper-backed catalogue of agricultural
implements he had picked up one day in the street. He liked to
look at the pictures of tractors, harvesters and rotary plows,
thinking what a great country America must be to have such
devices, when in China most grain was still beaten out with
bamboo rods on a stone threshing floor, and winnowed by being
thrown against the breeze. He hoped, after he had completed
his course at the university and the barbarians had been driven
back into the sea, to visit America and see these marvels for
himself. To see the Statue of Liberty, about which he had heard
so much. Mr. Barlow, the new chemistry instructor, had given

him a little replica of the statue, made of bronze. Ching amused himself sometimes, at night, by placing a lighted vesta match in the figure's torch, and pretending he was aboard a great liner, steaming up the harbor of New York. Some of the ignorant servants, observing this mysterious performance, decided the statue must be Ching's private god, which was indeed true although not in just the way they meant.

Week after week, through dust and mud and sunshine and storm, the caravan struggled on. At times, if the rain was especially heavy, Ching would take off his padded coat and add it to the straw mat that protected the load in his wheelbarrow. It made no difference if he got wet; books were a different matter. Like all Chinese, he had a deep reverence for the written or printed word. He knew that the Japanese must be barbarians, for everywhere they tried particularly to destroy libraries, pictures and other works of art. Their aim was to blot out Chinese culture, Dr. Wu-sung said.

The Doctor came up now, with Mr. Barlow, who had scarcely arrived in China to take his new post, before a terrific three-day bombardment from the air had caused the university to flee westward, as scores of similar institutions had done during the year. The exodus had made a deep impression on him; he was still complaining about it to Dr. Wu.

"But why bomb universities?" Ching heard him say, as the two strode along beside the wheelbarrow.

"The Japanese consider them military objectives," Dr. Wu, who spoke English perfectly, replied. "And quite rightly, too.

Our colleges and universities, teaching the doctrines of liberty, are among Japan's most dangerous foes. To them our new Mass Education Movement presents a serious problem. They do not want the Chinese people to learn what freedom means. It is wonderful how the spread of liberal ideas has inspired the youth of our nation. Madame Chiang Kai-shek is partly responsible for it. A splendid woman. You saw some of her police girls, I think, in Hangchow? She has organized groups of traveling players, high-school students, who loyally go about the country encouraging the people with patriotic dramas and songs. The spirit of resistance everywhere in China is very high."

"I should think these constant bombings," Mr. Barlow said, "would have broken public morale."

"The Chinese are a stubborn race." Dr. Wu's eyes sparkled. "I do not wish to boast, but we have successfully resisted the power of Japan for over four years. We have lost several million men. We have seen our women and children slaughtered, our finest cities taken, our richest provinces overrun . . . yet our spirit remains unbroken. None of the conquered nations of Europe was forced to endure so much, yet they surrendered. China fights on. Our young men and women are more determined than ever to win their battle for liberty, for democracy. I am proud of my people . . . very proud."

"You have reason to be," Mr. Barlow said quickly. "They have made great sacrifices. We in America have been lucky. We still hope to keep out of war."

"A very natural feeling." Dr. Wu nodded, his face grave. "War is stupid, senseless, a relic of barbarism. We in China have known that for a very long time. Unfortunately, however, it is not always possible to prevent war from being forced upon you. Peace cannot be had for the asking. Like other blessings, it may have to be fought for. The people of America have enjoyed a fortunate position. They have not lived next door to neighbors who insisted upon civilizing them with machine guns and bombs."

Ching, hearing a far-off drone in the air, like the buzzing of bees, glanced up. Three dark specks, flying low and incredibly fast, were approaching from the east. Some peasants working in a muddy rice field beside the road went calmly on with their labors. The caravan moved ahead, not changing its pace.

"They come close, Honorable Doctor," Ching said. "It may be they have learned what we carry. Would it not be better to leave the road?"

Dr. Wu glanced at the oncoming planes, then at the fields along the roadside. Rice paddies, crisscrossed with ditches. No refuge there for carts and wagons, with their heavy loads; they must stay where they were. But the human elements of the caravan might scatter. Dr. Wu called out a loud command, taken up at once by others along the straggling line. Grasping Mr. Barlow by the arm, he hurried from the road.

Most of the teachers and students did likewise, but the drivers of the wagons remained coolly with their teams, lest the animals, frightened by the sound of explosions, try to run away.

Ching calmly sat down on top of his loaded wheelbarrow. If the Japanese used machine guns, the spectroscope and the books might still be safe.

The three planes, flying so low that the faces of their pilots could be plainly seen, swept forward, one directly over the road, the other two covering the fields on either side of it, now spotted with figures moving singly and in groups. Bursts of machine-gun fire churned up the muddy rice paddies and scored the harder surface of the road. Ching felt wind ruffle his hair, leaped to his feet as the loaded barrow sank swiftly beneath him, its single wheel splintered by a bullet. The planes flew on, dropping no bombs. In the fields several motionless figures were lying. Nearby a bullock and a shaggy pony had collapsed in the shafts.

Dr. Wu came up, supporting a wounded student, a girl of sixteen; she had been shot through the thigh. Ching helped him lift the girl into one of the wagons, from which an elderly Chinese professor with bandaged feet at once descended to make room. Two porters and a middle-aged instructor lay dead in the fields; several others had been wounded. Groups of students ran to help them, to give first aid. A woman doctor was already bandaging the leg of the girl in the wagon, and drivers were removing the dead bullock to the roadside, where it would be cut up for food. The pony was not badly injured; a bullet had creased its shoulder. Everything moved smoothly, efficiently; the caravan was well organized after its journey of almost a thousand miles.

Ching watched the sky, thinking the warplanes might come back. Far off he saw them circle around, heading toward the east. The raid, then, had been merely a small Japanese pleasantry, a demonstration of frightfulness against fleeing refugees. He felt sure that had the raiders known the caravan's nature they would have returned and tried to destroy it.

Mr. Barlow was staring ruefully at the collapsed wheelbarrow.

"We can't leave the spectroscope," he said. "Or Professor Wu's books."

"No." Ching glanced along the road. The caravan was already in motion, with groups of students pulling the stranded wagon, carrying the packs of the dead porters, helping to transport the four huge quarters into which the carcass of the bullock had been divided. The bodies of the porters were left lying in the fields, surrounded by chattering peasants; that of the killed instructor had been placed in one of the carts. Evening was approaching; it was imperative to move quickly, to find a suitable camping place for the night.

"Well?" Mr. Barlow asked, as Ching tossed aside the fragments of the splintered wheel.

"I think, Honorable Sir," Ching said, "that we must carry it"—he waved toward the wheelbarrow—"at least so far as the camp." Crouching down, he raised the front of the barrow upon his shoulders. "If you will now take the handles, please."

The load was a heavy one but between them they managed it. Half a mile farther on, at the junction with a crossroad, they came to a burned and deserted village. Ching, catching sight of an object in the ditch, asked Mr. Barlow to stop, to ease their burden down.

When it had been deposited upon a stone-paved area beside the road, Ching crossed to the ditch, dragged something from the ashes and mud. It was an overturned wheelbarrow, with both handles broken off short but its wheel still intact. A moment later he was busy shoring up the front of their own barrow and fitting the new wheel in place.

Mr. Barlow, while waiting, amused himself by poking about in the ditch beneath the abandoned barrow, where a few small objects remained as mute evidence of hurried flight. A wooden rice bowl, with a single chopstick; a child's doll, its painted head crushed; a small, flat object wrapped in mud-stained silk. Removing the wrapper, Mr. Barlow drew out a square, paper-covered package the front of which bore a design strangely familiar to him. Gilt dragons, against a background of brilliant red. Firecrackers. He had handled many a similar pack, in times past.

Ching, glancing up from his work on the wheel, nodded.

"Here in China, Honorable Instructor," he said, "they are used on New Year's Day, and also at funerals. Ignorant persons believe that such noises frighten evil spirits away."

"In America," Mr. Barlow replied, smiling at Ching's efforts to instruct him, "we set them off to celebrate the Fourth of July. That, you know, is the day when we declared our independence. Tomorrow, as a matter of fact. I shall use them for a little private celebration." He opened the package, and detaching one of the small red cylinders, began to search his pockets for a match.

"Here, please," Ching said, producing his treasured vestas.

Mr. Barlow struck one of the small wax matches, holding the limp wick of the firecracker in its flame. The fuse, however, refused to burn. He tried a second and a third, only to see them sputter weakly out. Dampness had evidently done its work. Disappointed, he tossed the pack aside.

"Duds," he muttered. "No use."

Ching retrieved the package, thrusting it inside his shirt.

"It may be," he said, "that this ignorant one can dry them out." He stood up, removed the chocks from under the wheelbarrow. "If you please, now we can start."

Just beyond the village, sounds of marching feet came from around a sharp bend in the road, and a few moments later a company of soldiers appeared. Muscular, sun-tanned young men, some wearing dusty, blue-gray uniforms, others in padded jackets. They carried rifles over their shoulders, and upon their backs blankets, hand grenades, sacks of rice or millet. A few also boasted long two-handed swords. Their leader, a tall, keen-eyed young man in his early twenties, talked with Ching for a few moments in their native tongue, then turned his little company from the main road into a lane that crossed it just beyond the village.

"Guerilla soldiers," Ching said, grasping the handles of his wheelbarrow. "He—their captain—said our people are camped at an abandoned farm, half a mile farther on. Wanted to know what became of the airplanes. I told him they had gone back toward the east. He turned into the side road, I think, because of the trees along it; his men can march in single file under them and not be so easily seen from the air."

Mr. Barlow nodded and he and Ching went up the long hill. At the top of it they came to the deserted farm, once a prosperous place, to judge from the number and size of the buildings grouped within its walled courtyard. Besides the main dwelling there were several smaller ones for the accommoda- tion of servants, retainers, and a stable and storehouses along the rear wall. The sun was setting just as Ching and Mr. Bar- low reached the top of the hill; under its low rays the tiled roofs of the buildings gleamed like gold.

The wagons and other vehicles had been drawn up in the center of the courtyard, and the animals taken away to be watered and fed. Dr. Wu, on the lookout for his precious load of books, told Ching and Mr. Barlow that the owner of the property must have left in a great hurry, for the storehouses contained much food. An agreeable odor of roast bullock's flesh came from the kitchens. Ching, who was hungry, gave a pleased sniff. Not often did the little caravan enjoy a really bountiful meal. At some of the towns and villages Girl Scouts or units of the Y. M. C. A. had appeared to give them hot tea, boiled millet, rice or bean curds, but very rarely had they eaten any meat. Refugees from the coastal cities, streaming westward by the million, had swept the country well-nigh bare of food.

When the meal was over, Ching spent two hours helping to carry books, records and the more delicate pieces of equip- ment into the house. If, as everyone hoped, the caravan could stay camped where it was until the wounded had been healed, these things would be safer under roof. Not until quite late in the evening did Ching remember Mr. Barlow's firecrackers, his proposed celebration of the Fourth of July, next day.

The embers of a small fire glowed redly before the servants' quarters. Ching knelt down beside it, holding the pack over the coals. It would be very nice, he thought, to surprise Mr. Barlow with them in the morning.

Presently he tried one of the crackers. To his delight it ex- ploded with such a fierce bang that two of the porters came running out, wide-eyed, thinking the place had been attacked.

Grinning, Ching put the package in his pocket, started to- ward the main house, and bed. Over the wall of the courtyard he could make out the road, a winding pale ribbon leading to- ward the east, with fields and rice paddies bordering it on either side. The hill on which the farm stood was practically bare of trees. In the distance Ching could see a group of shadows, marking the ruins of the burned and gutted village.

He was about to turn to the house when his sharp eyes made out two pinpoints of light, advancing toward the village from the east. Another pair followed them, a short distance in the rear, and then a third, moving slowly through the gloom.

Motor cars, Ching decided. Japanese, perhaps, although ex- cept for the three low-flying planes there had been nothing to indicate that the enemy was so close behind. Still, few Chinese had cars, or the gasoline needed to run them, and the barbarian devils were constantly stretching out exploring fingers through the countryside—detachments of men in armored trucks, striking at communication points, bringing up ammunition and other supplies. Should enemy troops reach the farmhouse, discover the precious store of books and other equipment piled up there, all would be destroyed. Then an even more terrible thought crossed Ching's mind. Suppose the black war-birds, the evil vultures that had flown over the caravan in the road, had sent back word of its presence by radio, and so brought these motor trucks up?

The moving points of light hesitated, then stopped altogether near the center of the ruined village. Ching breathed easier; he had been afraid they might come on. If this meant that the trucks had decided to halt there for the night, the caravan might be able to pack up, move on before morning. Take refuge perhaps in some little-traveled side road, until the danger had passed. It was necessary, vitally necessary, to find out at once. Shaking with excitement, Ching ran swiftly down the hill.

His feet, in their soft felt slippers, made no sound, but as a turn in the road revealed the two staring headlights of the first car he fled into the adjoining rice field, moving more slowly now since he was up to his knees in water and mud.

A wide circle brought him to the edge of the village, where the ground was once more firm. He crept softly through heaps of ashes, past ruined homes, and came at last to what had once been an ancient *yamen*, with a walled garden, and a half-burned gilt-and-lacquered gateway, leading to the single main street.

Breathless, Ching peered through the sagging gate. In the road outside three trucks stood in a row, bulking huge and menacing in the darkness.

On a cobbled square opposite them a score of men were grouped about a small fire, with others sitting nearby. Ching could see only part of the square, since the trucks blocked his view. Some of the men were eating. Others were bent over what looked like a map. All were in uniform, and from the shape of their helmets and their height Ching knew them to be Japanese.

He crouched trembling behind one of the ancient gateposts, wondering what they planned to do. Having eaten, were they now about to move on? Or did they mean to camp here for the night? Several of the men spread blankets, stretched out on the cobbles. Others sat by the fire, talking and smoking. Possibly they merely intended to rest for an hour and then resume their journey. One of the group began to pace slowly up and down, a rifle over his shoulder.

Ching stood thinking, unable to decide what his next move should be. If he were to run back, warn the others of their danger, the Japanese, if they came on within the next hour or two, would surprise the caravan in the middle of its preparations to escape. Yet if the escape were not made, and the soldiers remained in the village all night, they could not fail to see the loaded carts and wagons in the courtyard when they passed

the farmhouse in the morning. Either course might spell disaster.

A third plan began to take form in his mind; a plan filled
with peril. Yet was it not a man's duty to make sacrifices, any
sacrifices, for his people, his country? Why not try in some way
to disable the trucks? Put them out of action? Then the miser-
able barbarians could not proceed at all! And the lamps of
knowledge might still be kept burning.

At first thought the plan seemed an impossible one, with that
keen-eyed sentry pacing up and down only a few yards away.
But was he keen-eyed? Ching had heard that many of these
small, apelike invaders had poor eyesight, were obliged to wear
glasses. Also, now that the fire had died down to a few glowing
embers, the street was very dark. Ching felt sure that were he
to creep through the gate, advance toward the line of trucks,
he could not be seen, since they would protect him from view
of the men on the other side.

Moving without sound, he tried it. In a moment he had
reached the side of the third truck. Across the road he could
make out the sentry, calmly pacing his beat.

Except for some knapsacks and a machine gun, the third
truck was empty. Motorized equipment, he realized, used for
transporting men. He felt its tires. Solid, as he had feared. No
chance to cut them, to put the car out of service that way. He
moved on to the second truck in the line, found it identical
with the one behind, except that a collection of intrenching
tools, shovels and picks, replaced the machine gun. Across the

street talk grew louder; the clump-clump of the sentry's boots had ceased; there was a sound of moving men.

Ching hurried to the third truck, the first in the line. The body of it seemed filled with rice straw—a most unlikely cargo —intended, no doubt, to conceal things of greater value beneath. He ran his hand through the straw, discovered that the truck was filled with rows of boxes, very heavy boxes containing, beyond question, rifle and machine-gun cartridges, or perhaps hand grenades in the larger ones. Forward, under the front seat of the car, stood rows of cans. From their feel and shape, Ching knew they were cans of gasoline. He had handled many, in the past, while driving the small station wagon used at the university to bring in supplies. Despite the increasing commotion across the road, he grinned, for now his plan of action had suddenly become clear!

Lifting out one of the cans he unscrewed its metal cap, poured the gasoline over the bundles of straw. A second and third quickly followed; then Ching stepped back. As the fumes rose, a strong odor of gasoline filled the air. In three steps he reached the shelter of the gateway. However deficient in eyesight the Japanese might be, they did not lack a sense of smell.

Conversation across the street suddenly ceased. Someone barked a harsh order. Ching drew the bunch of firecrackers and the box of vesta matches from his pocket. In spite of the rush of feet across the roadway his fingers were quite steady. He lit the main fuse of the small red package, tossed it sputtering into the truck. Then he turned and ran.

"Off with you . . . we'll take care of these apes."

As the firecrackers reached the mass of gasoline-soaked straw, a blinding explosion almost knocked Ching from his feet. The ruins of the village were lit by a sheet of flame. The light of it showed creeping figures coming toward him—tall, muscular figures, armed with rifles and two-handed swords. Another explosion came, and still another, as the boxes of ammunition began to feel the fierce heat of the blaze.

A hard hand fell on Ching's shoulder, whirling him about. He stared up into the face of the guerilla leader with whom he had spoken several hours earlier on the road. Recognizing him, the young officer's frown relaxed.

"On with you!" he growled. "Tell your people they are safe! We will take care of these apes!" An instant later he and his men were charging toward the line of trucks.

Ching ran up the road. Behind him the sky was lit by endless explosions, as boxes of hand grenades were set off and white-hot cans of gasoline burst with tremendous roars, scattering their contents high in the air. He hurried on, breathless, a little regretful as well that Mr. Barlow would not now have any firecrackers with which to celebrate his country's Independence Day.

At the top of the hill he found the chemistry instructor standing with Dr. Wu. About them were gathered a crowd of students, all peering excitedly toward the distant village. Dr. Wu seized him by the arm.

"What's all this?" he asked sharply. "What has happened?"

Panting, Ching tried to explain.

"I was afraid the barbarians would come and . . . and de-stroy all our books . . . our instruments!" he stammered, "so I . . . I blew up their ammunition truck. Now the guerilla soldiers are there, to . . . to finish." He turned to Mr. Barlow. "I am sorry, Honorable Sir, that I was forced to use the fire-crackers, leaving none for your celebration tomorrow."

Mr. Barlow seemed for a moment puzzled, then he glanced quickly at the luminous dial of his watch. "Not tomorrow, Ching!" he shouted gaily. "Today! It's past midnight! Today is the Fourth of July," he went on to Dr. Wu, "and"—his eyes sought the sky over the village, still filled with bursting stars—"that's just about the finest lot of fireworks I've ever seen!"

Ching smiled, greatly pleased. Dr. Wu patted him on the shoulder.

"Good boy!" he said. "You have done China a splendid ser-vice . . . and saved my books! At all costs the lamps of knowl-edge must be kept burning!"

From the Far East, where the people of China stood bravely defending their ancient homeland against a savage foe, I turned my eyes Westward, to see the democracies of Europe lying prostrate, their banners of freedom trailing in the dust. One by one small, peaceful nations, defenseless because of the high ideals of civilization they maintained, had by force and treachery been blotted out.

All Europe was dark, shrouded in dreadful night; a night filled with cries of anguish from victims in bombed cities, from tortured prisoners in concentration camps, from millions of once-free men and women forced to hard labor as slaves of their self-appointed masters. Through the darkness crept ghosts of plundered nations . . . of Austria, Czechoslovakia and Poland, of Norway, Denmark and Holland, of Albania, Finland and the Baltic States, of Belgium and of France. The roar of bursting bombs, the rattle of machine guns, the tramp of marching men drowned the appeals of those who were starving, while the air lanes screamed ever new and increasing demands on the part of the victors, from rescue of oppressed minorities and more living room to destruction of all democracies and extermination of the Jews. A hideous roar of false propaganda, designed to cloak their one real purpose, conquest . . . domination of the world. A New Order was to be set up, based on cruelty, treachery, force . . . the order of the jungle.

Upon a shell-torn beach at Dunkirk I saw the democracies of Europe dying. Only across a narrow strip of water did men still have faith to hold their heads high, to face death itself rather than sacrifice their freedom, their honor, their belief in God and the truth.

THE BEACH AT DUNKIRK

IT WAS a dismal day; there had been rain during the night, and the roads and fields of northern France were sodden and heavy with mud.

Steve Hunter turned from the ambulance, parked under a dripping poplar tree, and shook his head.

"No soap," he muttered. "Tank's dry as a bone."

Mary Giffen, the blue-eyed nurse from Cincinnati, button-holed a young British officer hurrying along the crowded road. He listened to her patiently, trying to smile.

"Petrol?" he said vaguely. "Can't say, really. Old duffer back at the crossroads, keeps the Three Rabbits, had a few tins last night. Probably gone now. Sorry." He plodded on.

Steve glanced at the stalled car.

"I'll go," he said. "We've got to get out of here, quick."

For a moment he listened, staring down the road. Far to the south bright flashes, a rumble of artillery fire indicated that the enemy was coming close. He drew back under the trees as a plane droned overhead. By the deep note of its engines he knew the visitor to be German. The sky was full of them, now that the Belgians had thrown down their arms. He hoped they would respect the red cross so plainly painted on the ambulance's top, but from past experience he doubted it.

The small tavern and store at the crossroads was a good three miles away. Steve took a short cut over the fields, running, ankle deep in mud. By the time he came within sight of the *estaminet* he knew he would get no gas there. The droning bomber had dropped an evil egg, and the Three Rabbits had disappeared in a cloud of smoke and dust.

Well, that was that. He started back, cursing his luck. A regiment of French infantry was streaming toward him, over a muddy beet field, blocking the way. He turned to the road, found it, too, choked with tanks, lorries, retreating troops. The firing off to the south sounded nearer, now. The enemy was advancing steadily, in spite of heroic resistance. Only the day before he had heard how a Scottish regiment, the Green Howards, had thrown back an entire German division, charging savagely with the bayonet. The Nazis didn't like cold steel, but . . . this war wasn't being fought with bayonets.

No sign of the ambulance crew. Steve wondered what had become of them, hoping Mary Giffen would not think she and the others had been deserted. As driver of the ambulance he felt responsible for getting them out. Well—a fellow couldn't do more than his best; even with gas, there'd have been mighty little chance of escape, with the roads jammed solid from ditch to ditch, and the fields hub-deep in mud.

He stared at the passing sea of faces, hoping he might recognize the members of his crew. A roar of motors, close at hand, announced the presence of a hedgehopping plane. It came on, sweeping the crowded road with bursts of machine-gun fire. A red-faced Tommy, taking cool aim, picked off the pilot with a lucky rifle shot, and the plane crashed not fifty feet from where Steve stood. He watched the Tommy and his companions drag a machine gun from the wreckage and set it up on the rear of an empty ammunition truck, stalled in the ditch. Another low-flying Stuka, greeted with an unexpected blast from the gun, zoomed off, trailing clouds of black smoke.

A British officer whom Steve knew came along the roadside, his face gray with pain, one arm, limp, dripping blood. Steve went up to him, producing miraculously a roll of gauze.

"Lucky I had this in my pocket," he said. "Shed your coat and I'll fix up that arm." He ignored the officer's protests, that the wound was a "mere scratch." "See anything of my ambulance crew?" Steve went on. "I've lost touch."

"Yes. They went off with some of our stretcher-bearers. In a lorry. Toward the coast."

"Ought to be safe then." Steve, finished his first aid operations, helped the young officer on with his tunic and improvised a sling for his arm. "Guess I'd best head that way myself." He started off, brushing aside the Britisher's thanks. "It's my job, that's all."

He kept to the fields, feeling sure he'd make better progress in spite of the mud than by the crowded roads. So his little crew was out of the mess, if not out of danger. Well, that was something. In a couple of hours they should reach the coast. He figured it wasn't more than twenty miles away. On foot he'd be longer. Most of the night, he guessed.

Tough going, through these fields of sugar beets and young grain, but the rumble and roar of battle, coming ever nearer, drove him on. Far off to the left he could see a ribbon of road, black with refugees and troops. At this distance they looked like toiling ants, with hungry birds swooping down from over-head.

Darkness came, to blot out the sight; darkness except for vivid flashes, like heat lightning, in the southern sky. Steve plodded on, soaked to the skin as a result of wading through innumerable small canals and irrigation ditches that traversed the low, flat fields. When at last dawn lit up the east, it showed all the country ahead being flooded, as though from hastily opened dykes. He splashed through water ankle-deep and hourly rising, wondering how long it would be before he reached the coast. A great plume of smoke, lit up by bursts of flame, hung over the northern horizon, marking the location of the port.

Steve thought that as long as he lived he would never forget his first sight of stricken Dunkirk. The bomb-shattered dwell-

ings, crumbling to heaps of gray dust. The dazed and sobbing
people, wandering through crater-pitted streets. The blazing
warehouses, blasted docks, surrounding a harbor littered with
half-sunken wrecks of ships, smoke-blackened hulks from which
still rose occasional wisps of flame. The sky above, filled with
darting airplanes; and, most poignant of all, the endless throngs
of troops, streaming toward the devastated harbor and the
beach.

Long columns of soldiers, men of different races—English
and French for the most part—but with them Belgians and
Czechs, Dutchmen and Poles, even an occasional group of Nor-
wegians, brave men all, fighting for freedom despite the bitter
fate that had overtaken their homelands, holding their heads
high even in this hour of defeat.

The water in the harbor, the channel beyond, was churned
white by exploding bombs, as heavy German planes and their
escorting fighters battled with the swift, furiously driven craft
of the Royal Air Force. Steve, watching the savage combat,
thought he had never before seen so many planes. The sky was
black with them. The sound of machine-gun fire, of bursting
bombs, filled the air with a continuous deafening roar.

Only one pier remained intact at the port; a long, slender
affair, scarcely wide enough to accommodate three men marching abreast. A British destroyer lay at the end of it, taking on
a thin column of troops. A salvo of bombs hurtled from the
sky and the destroyer slowly sank amid clouds of steam and
smoke.

"Blimey!" Steve heard someone mutter beside him. "Looks like we missed the bus!" He turned to see a line of Tommies marching by, shoulder to shoulder as if on parade.

Another destroyer edged in alongside the pier, began to take on troops. A score of transports lay farther out but they drew too much water to approach nearer shore. A shallow, shifting beach stretched for several miles from Dunkirk westward toward La Panne; on it stood tens of thousands of men, waiting in silence for small boats from the ships to take them aboard. Many waded through the low surf, standing in water up to their shoulders; others swam farther, braving bombs and machine-gun fire to reach the approaching boats.

Steve went along the crowded, shell-torn beach, littered with broken-down trucks and cast-off equipment of every sort, from boxes of food and ammunition to knapsacks and guns. Overhead the bombers and combat planes swirled in chattering circles. Now and then bursts of machine-gun fire spattered the sands like leaden rain. The silent men closed up, gave the victims first aid. There was suffering, death on that tragic beach, but Steve saw no fear. It seemed to him that these waiting thousands had found a new courage, a deeper faith in their extremity. They were upheld by the resolute spirit that is the heritage of free men.

Things were different in battle. Then one fought back and died in hot blood. Here no blows could be struck in self-defense. It took courage of a higher order to stand hour after hour on a bare, unsheltered beach awaiting deliverance or death with chins up . . . not death that came quickly, but with slow, groping fingers, touching one here, passing his neighbor by unharmed. Now if ever was a time for broken discipline, for panic, yet Steve saw none. Everywhere about him he beheld only a fierce, unflinching pride . . . the pride of men who believed in their cause and were ready to die for it. Watching them, Steve was reminded of the immortal words of Patrick Henry. "Give me liberty or give me death!"

At his elbow two British officers were discussing a report that had just come in from Calais. A single regiment of Territorials had been left there with orders to hold back the enemy until the dykes could be opened, flooding the Dunkirk fields. The fields were flooded, now, and time so afforded for many more of the retreating forces to escape, but . . . of the defenders at Calais only a handful had survived, to be brought off by a British warship. Men could still die, it seemed, in a good cause, gallantly, unknown and unsung.

The throngs of men on the beach grew constantly larger, in spite of the efforts being made by the ships' boats to take them off. The enemy had boastfully announced, several days before, that the armies in northern France, many hundred thousand men, would be exterminated. Steve, watching the trickle being taken aboard the small boats, thought that the chances of escape for most of the others, including himself, were infinitesimal. . . . Nothing short of a miracle could save them.

And then, the miracle occurred. Over the horizon came a score of strange craft, vanguard of an ever-increasing fleet.

Steve rubbed his eyes, wondering if they had deceived him. A fleet made up of launches, fishing boats and river steamers, cabin cruisers, private yachts and wherries, coal barges, trawl-ers and tugs! On they came by scores and hundreds, all the business and pleasure craft of England's south ports, manned by old men and schoolboys, women and young girls, speeding to the aid of their beleaguered countrymen through a rain of enemy bombs, calm and unafraid. Gallantly they advanced, this strange armada, and Steve, with a lump in his throat, thought it a sight the like of which no man had ever before seen.

The waters off shore became a sea of bobbing heads as thou-sands of men waded beyond the breakers, to be dragged to safety. All along the coast as far as the eye could reach the work of rescue went on. Steve felt like cheering.

He went down to the line of surf, swimming out for per-haps a quarter of a mile. He was an excellent swimmer, but the water felt unexpectedly cold. Not far away a barge filled with dripping, shivering men was being towed along by a tug. Steve struck out toward it, using a powerful overhand stroke. When he was fifty yards away he heard the roar of airplane motors, saw a diving Stuka release a well-aimed bomb.

It struck the crowded barge amidships. At that short dis-tance, there was little chance to miss. In an instant the air was filled with flying bodies, splintered timbers, foam. Steve, seeing the bomb released, had the presence of mind to dive. When he came up both barge and tug had disappeared. Near him a soldier wearing French horizon blue was feebly struggling

Near him, a French soldier was feebly trying to keep afloat.

to keep afloat. With a few swift strokes Steve reached him, managing, by treading water, to prevent the man's head from going under.

The beat of a propeller, close by, made Steve turn. A small cabin cruiser was coming toward him, with an elderly, gray-haired gentleman at the wheel and a slim girl in sweater and slacks standing on its tiny foredeck. She shook a clenched fist at the sky, muttering the single word, "Beasts!"

The wounded Frenchman was conscious but seemed in great pain. From the dark spot on his tunic that slowly spread over a gash in the cloth, Steve thought a bomb-splinter had pierced his chest. The cabin cruiser came close and the girl, reaching down, caught the wounded soldier's collar in a firm grasp.

"Easy," she said. "We're a bit overloaded now." Steve, glancing up, saw two shivering figures crouched in the cockpit. There were others, he judged, in the small cabin; the rail of the craft was very close to the water. He helped get the wounded man aboard.

"Shall I come too?" he asked.

The girl turned to her companion at the wheel. He wore a blue peajacket with brass buttons and looked like an ex-naval man.

"We'll chance it, my dear," he said, glancing at the water. "But no more, or we shan't get back." He spun the wheel, turned the cruiser's bow northward.

The French soldier lay stretched out on the small forward deck, breathing heavily. Steve climbed aboard, taking care not to tip the overloaded craft too far. He opened the wounded man's tunic and shirt, saw the jagged wound in his chest. Bleeding was mostly internal; there was nothing he could do. This was a hospital case. They should reach shore, he thought, before nightfall.

"Just lie still," he said gently. "We'll land pretty soon and find you a doctor."

"Many thanks, *monsieur*," the man replied in excellent English. "I am grateful . . . but . . . it will be of little use, I fear."

Steve, who had seen such wounds before, said nothing. A trace of scarlet foam on the man's lips spoke volumes. He stared over the bow, saw a young fellow swimming toward them. He was in uniform and wore a flyer's helmet.

"Not much of a swimmer," he gasped, reaching for the rail. "Better . . . in the . . . air." Although exhausted he managed to grin. "I say, old chap, could you give me . . . a hand?"

Steve reached down, grasped the man's wrist. He seemed very young; scarcely out of his teens.

"Have you aboard in no time. . . ."

A voice came sharply from the wheel.

"Can't take any more!" the elderly steersman said. He spoke with regret, but firmly. "Overloaded now. Sorry."

Steve drew the young aviator to the rail.

"It's one of your flyers, sir," he called back. "You couldn't possibly leave him. I'm a good swimmer; he can have my place. Will you hold on to his wrist for a moment, miss?" Steve turned to the girl. "While I shed this wet coat and my shoes."

The young woman gave him a look of admiration, her deep blue eyes glowing.

"You're . . . splendid!" she whispered. "Splendid! This boy has been . . . fighting for us . . . risking his life. . . ."

"Of course, miss." Steve stripped off his heavy, water-soaked tunic. The Frenchman on the deck raised his head.

"No need, *monsieur* . . . *m'amzelle*," he gasped. "I am finished . . . done for! *Vive la France!*" His voice rang out triumphantly as he threw himself sideways over the rail.

Instinctively Steve plunged after him, feeling sure as he did so that they would not see the man again. With his lungs pierced, his breathing choked, he was certain to sink at once. Perhaps that was best. Why drag him back to hours of needless suffering . . . suffering which could have but one end? He had chosen to die gloriously, that another might live. What greater love hath any man . . . ?

Steve came to the surface, wiped the salt water from his eyes. The Frenchman had disappeared, leaving no trace. Fifty feet away the cruiser was slowly turning. One of the rescued men aboard had lifted the young flyer over the rail. Off to the right a bombed motorboat was sinking, her crew and passengers trapped in a sea of blazing oil. Steve turned his head away, swam toward the cabin cruiser.

He pulled himself to the deck, sat there, dripping. The girl came from the tiny cabin, carrying a cup of tea in her hand. Steve drank the steaming liquid gratefully; he felt chilled to the bone.

"That boy from the R. A. F. wishes to thank you," she said. "He'd been in the water over an hour and was about to go down. I'm trying to find him some dry clothes." Steve saw that she no longer wore her sweater. "You need some your-self," she went on. "But. . . ."

"I'll be all right." Steve gave her his empty cup. "That tea has fixed me fine."

The girl regarded him with a swift, appraising smile.

"You're an American, aren't you?" she said.

"Yep." Steve nodded. "Been driving an ambulance."

"I've met very few Americans." She seemed embarrassed. "Hardly any at all. We—my father and I—live very quietly in a small cottage near Dover. I teach school there. He can't get about much because of an injury. At Jutland, during the last war. You see he"—she hesitated, lowering her voice—"he lost both his legs."

Steve stared at the elderly man behind the wheel, astonished. So that was why he sat so still, his knees covered by a plaid shawl. It would have required courage for anyone to brave the Channel, to face a rain of bombs in this small craft; for a leg-less man and a young girl to attempt it was nothing short of heroic. He attempted to say so but the girl interrupted him.

"If we get back safely," she went on, "perhaps, sometime, you could come and see us. I . . . I'm Ellen Lodge." With a sudden bright color in her cheeks she turned away.

Steve sat gazing out over the water. A light breeze ruffled its surface, sent small waves hurrying along the cruiser's sides, perilously close to her rail. Should the breeze freshen materially by the time they reached mid-channel, those waves would come aboard the heavily loaded craft and probably sink her. Little chance for any of them, were that to happen. None at all, Steve thought, for a legless man.

Beyond the cruiser's stern he could see the French coast, almost hidden by a vast black pall of smoke. It seemed somehow symbolic of the pall of darkness that had fallen over Europe. A black cloud of treachery and ignorance, of cruelty and hate. Of violent action, preached to young men trained to be hard . . . trained to kill without compunction . . . trained to war. The schoolboys of a nation, forbidden to think, taught only to act. To inflict suffering on others, with the thoughtless cruelty of youth, neither knowing nor caring what the nature of such action might be, indifferent to its results. Boys with strong, sturdy bodies and warped and twisted minds, fed on doctrines of blood and iron, trained to cruel violence, marching to conquest hypnotized by the endless hollow clatter of their own hobnailed boots.

Steve glanced at the face of the silvery-haired man behind the wheel. Sensitive, yet strong; the face of a thinker as well as of a man of action. Kindly, in spite of its harsh lines of suffering. The type, Steve thought, to whom liberty would be a priceless possession and democracy a living and militant creed. Was it to older men like this, rather than to youth, he wondered, that the world must look for strength, for spiritual guidance in its hour of need? Men of mature mind, of broad vision, capable of thinking things through. Yet prompt to act when occasion demanded action? The older men of England had not hesitated to risk their lives on behalf of her sons, on this never-to-be-forgotten day. All about him Steve could see ships of the gallant rescue fleet, bringing home countless thousands snatched from the jaws of Dunkirk's Hell. He crept to the rear of the cockpit, spoke to the still figure at the wheel.

"Breeze seems to be going down, sir," he said.

"Yes." The gray-haired steersman gave him a quick look, his eyes very keen. "Usually does, with the sun, on bright days like this. I'd rather counted upon it. We should make port in an hour."

"Do you think," Steve went on, "that the Germans will attempt to cross the Channel?"

"It is their best opportunity . . . and England's darkest hour. Even if most of our men get out of France safely they'll have been forced to sacrifice their equipment. That means we're defenseless. For a time, at least. But we English are a determined, a stubborn people. We do not give up easily. Our faith is in God, and the right. We may suffer, even die, but I do not think we shall be conquered. No people can be, so long as love of freedom lives in their hearts. Love of freedom, and truth."

"What is truth?" Steve asked, smiling.

The gray-haired steersman's eyes snapped.

"It is something those violent young men of Herr Hitler, fed so long on lies, will some day have to learn. The great truth, preached on the Mount by a great teacher whom Pilate, too, affected to despise. I am a student of history, young man, and I tell you, without fear of contradiction, that never in the course of time has any man been truly great who lacked the quality of mercy, nor has any nation endured for long whose god was the god of force. You will see. We—my own people— have not always been perfect. In the past we have been guilty of many faults. But compared to what Herr Hitler and his henchmen are doing to the conquered nations of Europe today, we are angels. Look." He pointed across the water to the chalk cliffs of Dover, clear and brilliant against the evening sky. "Upon those cliffs the watchfires of liberty have burned for a thousand years! They will continue to burn, as long as civiliza- tion endures. The things we have stood for—honor, justice, law —are parts of the great truth. They can never be blotted out!" He glanced proudly around at the fleet of ships, large and small, that dotted the Channel; rusty tugs and tall-sparred yachts, river boats and coal barges, all moving steadily toward the homeland. The late sunlight covered them with a sheen of gold. From a battered trawler came the voices of men singing. The old gentleman raised his head, joined them. "There will always be an England!"

Steve, watching, saw in his face, his eyes, the fire of a deep and lasting faith . . . a faith that can move mountains. That could work such a miracle as he had seen today. That had given old men and children strength to move an army!

As the year of dreadful night drew to a close, I gazed in sorrow upon a stricken world. A world gripped by fear, trembling before the power of the lie. England still fought on in spite of blasted cities, sunken ships, but France lay helpless beneath the heel of a ruthless foe. The guardians of her liberty had slept upon the ramparts while traitors plotted destruction from within. With dismay I watched the passing of a proud nation, wondering that once again, through blood and suffering, men should be forced to learn the age-old lesson, that freedom is not merely a way of life to be enjoyed, but a citadel to be jealously guarded against enemies forever lying in wait at its gates.

Even in the great democracy of the west I saw men nodding while the world about them burned; heard voices confidently crying that the storm which had destroyed Europe could not cross an ocean to trouble them. Knowing the danger I held my torch high, but through the murk of falsehood and treachery, of cunning propaganda and childlike ignorance, many were unable to see its guiding flame.

Then I beheld the marvel of a small, weak people daring what greater nations lacked the courage to do. Men of Hellas, marching forth to defend their ancient altars against the boasted power of a self-styled Caesar. Proudly I watched them hurl back his legions from their mountain passes, as they once had hurled back the might of Persia, to preserve democracy for the world. Here in this brave land the flame of my torch had first been truly kindled; I prayed now that the fires blazing from Greek mountain tops might turn into a world-wide conflagration, by which tyranny and dishonor and the rule of brute force would be forever swept from the face of the earth.

My hopes and my prayers were in vain. Once more, from the heights of the Acropolis, I saw the fires of freedom blotted out by the forces of evil. Over the noble ruins of the Parthenon, where men once worshipped beauty and truth, I watched them hang the black banner of cruelty, injustice, hate. Soon dictators, fighting between themselves, were drenching the soil of Russia with the blood of countless more millions. All around me I saw only misery, starvation, death.

From the desecrated ruins of the Parthenon I turned my eyes to the West. There, too, men had built a temple dedicated to liberty, to government by the people for the people. Its white dome rose proudly against the sky. The flag that flew above that dome had never yet been lowered in any hour that endangered freedom's cause. I took heart, believing that no power from within or without could force it to be lowered now. Yet seeing what had happened to other free men, I trembled, for I knew the time was short.

TORCH OF LIBERTY

STEVE HUNTER rose abruptly from the smoking-room table, went out on deck. Remarks by one of the men with whom he had been sitting left him fighting mad. A glib-tongued young fellow from the Middle West named Martin—Peter Martin—who had been studying art in Paris but was now on his way home because he found conditions in France under Nazi rule "a bit too trying."

What enraged Steve particularly was the young man's contemptuous remarks about America. About democracy. Pure bunk, he said, to claim that everyone was born equal. Such ideas might be all very well, in theory, but in practice they didn't work out. It was common knowledge that a few rich men controlled the industry of the nation through special privilege; that business was a racket, and politics a rotten graft. The

United States, he thought, should make peace with the dictators; then he could go back to France, where people knew how to live. "But not to die, apparently," Steve had snapped, as he left the table. They knew how to die in England, he thought, after the things he had seen during the past five months in London.

He strode along the deck, frowning. It shocked and disgusted him to hear an American speak in such terms of his own country, especially when he was scuttling back to it from Europe in search of safety.

The refugee ship was making rather slow progress up the harbor, owing to an early morning mist. Passengers from many lands crowded the rails, eager to catch their first glimpse of New York, of the Statue of Liberty. Even the dozen or more English children, usually to be seen romping about the decks, were now grouped in a silent huddle forward, staring into the gray curtain of fog. Steve nodded to one of them, smiling. A slim, sad-eyed lad of fifteen, Alec Hutchinson, who had lost both parents in one of London's endless bombing raids. Since his escape from Dunkirk, Steve had been doing volunteer relief work there, driving an ambulance in the devastated East End. He had seen suffering and horror unbelievable, and courage on the part of simple, homey working folks before which any more fortunate man might have stood ashamed.

He watched the faces of the people crowding the ship's rail. Some smiled; others brushed frank tears from their eyes. All, Steve thought, were upheld by a hope which while deep was still reluctant, as though they feared that *this* refuge too, like others they had sought, might prove to be only an illusion. Denmark, Norway, Holland, France, the Balkan countries . . . they also had seemed safe harbors of freedom, in the not-distant past.

Steve had talked with many of these unfortunates on the way over, had heard their tragic stories. There was the elderly Frenchwoman, whose husband, a famous physician, had shot himself on the day Nazi troops marched into Paris. The Czech dramatist was still weak and haggard after his eight terrible months in a concentration camp. The little old lady from Amsterdam had rowed herself and her invalid husband across the Channel in a twelve-foot boat, only to see him killed in an air-raid. The Polish violinist, a young Jew, had been driven by the Nazi fury from four conquered countries, and now sought only the right to live. Sad, broken people who regarded Steve doubtfully when he assured them that they would need no ration cards in New York to get such things as sugar, coffee, and butter, and that they could listen to the radio as they pleased without fear of arrest by the secret police, since in America there were no secret police.

The fog showed signs of lifting but it still hid the tall buildings of the city from view. Steve went forward, standing beside the rail. His months in London had been a ghastly nightmare in spite of the indomitable courage shown by the people. He was glad to be coming home, to peace, to sanity. England was making a brave fight against desperate odds, defending the last stronghold of European democracy, but he was oppressed by the fear that she too might go down before the totalitarian storm. As for the Continent, conditions there were appalling. He knew, because a stream of refugees, making their way by underground channels, constantly arrived in London with stories that shocked men's souls. Of France, tricked, plundered, despoiled, her youth in prison or labor camps, her people facing famine, disease, death. Of Poland, her leading men executed, and millions starved in a deliberate and systematic attempt to exterminate a once-proud race. Of Holland, Czechoslovakia, Norway, France, even Greece and her Balkan neighbors, looted, starved, driven to desperation by a brutal Gestapo, seething with revolt. A vast force of evil, he felt, had been let loose upon the world; a force of destruction, based on man's lowest, most savage instincts—criminal instincts that civilized society had for two thousand years tried to suppress, to stamp out.

He peered ahead through the gloom. It was like coming to another planet to be home. Here in America people had at least tried to live up to certain ideals. Not always successfully, perhaps, but they had tried. The ideals of thinking, civilized men, such as Washington, Jefferson, Lincoln—men with nobility of soul, capable of understanding such things as honor, justice, reason. A nation, he thought, instinctively reflected in its actions the spirit of its leaders. The forces of intolerance, of cruelty, now rolling over Europe, deaf to all human decencies, reflected only the moral bankruptcy of those who led them—

In England people knew how to die . . .

common, ignorant men, power-mad, seeking to remake the world upon their own vulgar pattern. Steve shuddered, remembering the horrors of London. Could that dark flood of intolerance, of evil roll across three thousand miles of sea?

A hand, touching his arm, woke him from these unhappy reveries. He looked down to find the English boy, Alec Hutchinson, standing at his elbow. Less than a month before Steve had helped to drag him, suddenly orphaned, from a mass of blazing ruins.

"Yes, Alec?" he said.

"When shall we reach New York, sir?" the boy asked.

"Very soon." Steve put his arm about the youngster's shoulders. "If it weren't for the mist, we could see the city now. Look! Over there!" Steve pointed. Above the thinning fog rose New York's high towers, like white, gleaming ramparts in the morning sun. Ramparts of freedom, of democracy, he felt, to be defended at all costs . . . not by lip service, by flag-waving, but by strong arms, and stern, unwavering faith in ideals worth more than life itself . . . ideals that were a priceless heritage.

The English boy stood for a moment staring ahead.

"They . . . they're so high!" he murmured. "Towers! All white and gold! Like a fairy castle in a dream . . . !"

"Part of a dream, anyway, Alec," Steve said solemnly. "Perhaps the most beautiful one ever conceived by man. A dream of people, of a nation, not only physically but mentally and spiritually free. To live, to work, to achieve . . . to make their dreams come true. Democracy—the kind we've tried to build in America—isn't just a political institution giving everyone the right to vote. It's more than that; much more. A way of life designed to liberate not only men's bodies, but their souls. You'll understand better, son, after you've lived over here a while."

"I think I do now, sir . . . a bit. We have much the same sort of thing in England . . . or had, until the Nazis came. My father"—the boy choked for a moment, then went on— "my father used to read to me, nights . . . history. About . . . Magna Carta, and the Roman Republic and Greece. He said democracy was easier to carry on in small nations, like the Greek city-states, where the people could meet together and talk over their problems, than in big countries such as the British Empire, or yours here in the United States."

"He was quite right, Alec. Modern civilization progresses year after year in a huge, ever-expanding spiral. Not only upward but outward as well. That means the problems, the responsibilities of each generation become greater, as the frontiers of democracy become wider, more difficult to defend. They can't be defended, successfully, unless the people of a nation— all the people—are united. By the same hopes, the same ideals, the same deep, burning faith. . . ."

"Almost like a religion, sir. My father used to say that, too. He claimed democracy *was* a religion, same as the one taught by Christ. You see what I mean, sir. Kindness, brotherhood, giving the other fellow a chance. He—my Dad—wasn't very well educated, but he read a lot. Isn't it about time, sir, we were seeing the Statue of Liberty?"

"Why . . . yes." Steve glanced about the mist-enshrouded harbor, pointed to a dark object looming above the haze off the ship's port bow. "Over there. You can just see her head and shoulders, her arm. . . ."

He stopped suddenly, feeling his heart leap. The morning sun, bursting through the thin curtain of fog, lit up the harbor like a gigantic spotlight. Brilliant rays, striking full upon the great statue, turned its dull bronze to living flame.

"Oh!" the English boy gasped. "It . . . it's all shining like . . . like fire. . . !"

"A Pillar of Fire!" Steve muttered. "Let's hope, Alec, it will always stand there, to enlighten the world. That's what it was originally called, you know—Liberty Enlightening the World. Guiding men's footsteps in the path of reason, justice, peace." The thrill that the sudden appearance of the statue had brought was still with him. He made a stern resolve to do all in his power that the horrors he had seen abroad might never come to this great, free country . . . Here was the last stronghold of liberty. Her torch must be kept blazing high above the murk, the fog which had darkened so large a part of the earth.

"Is . . . is it made of gold, sir?" he heard Alec ask at his elbow.

"Why, yes, son," he said. "In a way. Pure gold. Like most precious things. Including the truth."

EPILOGUE

I am the Spirit of Liberty. By the light of my torch all who wander blindly in the shadows of fear and oppression can be set free.

But not unless they have wisdom to see the truth, and courage to fight and even to die for it.

Let no man think that liberty is his unless the flame that lights my torch shall burn with equal brilliance inside his breast.

I bring the blessing of freedom to those who serve me, not with careless words and the waving of banners, but with toil and sweat and blood and tears.

So was it gained during the long, hard years of the past: so must it ever be defended and preserved.

That is the lesson I bring you, as I have learned it through twenty centuries. Guard well my temple, O free men of today, lest, like the Parthenon of old, it too may lie in ruins beneath a Conqueror's cruel flag.

www.ingramcontent.com/pod-product-compliance
Lightning Source LLC
Chambersburg PA
CBHW071314090426
42738CB00012B/2702